T0353095

HAUNTED
SOMERSET

HAUNTED
SOMERSET

JOHN GARLAND

First published 2007

Reprinted in 2008 by The History Press

The Mill, Brimscombe Port,
Stroud, Gloucestershire, GL5 2QG
www.thehistorypress.co.uk

Reprinted 2010

© John Garland, 2007

The right of John Garland to be identified as the Author
of this work has been asserted in accordance with the
Copyrights, Designs and Patents Act 1988.

All rights reserved. No part of this book may be reprinted
or reproduced or utilised in any form or by any electronic,
mechanical or other means, now known or hereafter invented,
including photocopying and recording, or in any information
storage or retrieval system, without the permission in writing
from the Publishers.

British Library Cataloguing in Publication Data.
A catalogue record for this book is available from the British Library.

ISBN 978 0 7524 4335 5

Typesetting and origination by Tempus Publishing.
Printed and bound in England.

CONTENTS

Acknowledgements

I especially wish to thank my editor Nicola Guy for her supportive guidance while I was compiling this collection. I dedicate these pages to June Copp for her time and knowledge of Dunster Castle's invisible occupants and ghost connoisseur Ian Gibson-Small. All photographs, unless otherwise stated, are by Jon Dathen.

THIS WORLD AND THAT: AN INTRODUCTION

The phantoms in this book are allegedly factual, and any of them attempting to perform outside of its pages will be rebuked for their rudeness!

Ghosts light up a flutter of memories. Flowing through the centuries, Somerset's ghosts and ghouls have been celebrated in folk song, oral yarns, superstitions and of course, most controversial of all, reports of their unwelcome arrival. The spirit world, in essence, revolves around exits and entrances; they come and go, and have been the focus of many a book by renowned novelists, poets and short-fiction writers. Among the many enduring story tellers, the French author Guy de Maupassant knew how to craft a compelling page turner. And if you have ever met or sensed 'something' from the invisible realities, then you will enjoy this affinity with the supernatural from *Clochette*:

> They are strange things, these old memories that haunt our minds and will not be dismissed. This is such an old one, so old that I cannot understand why it remains in my mind so vividly and so tenaciously. I have seen so many sinister things, so many moving and terrible things since, that it astonishes me to find that I cannot pass a day, one single day, without a vision of Mother Clochette appearing before me in her habit as I knew her once upon a time, so long ago, when I was ten or twelve years old.

But, Somerset has her own immortal writers and poets who have recounted, reported and retold some of the county's haunted history. The late and inimitable prose of Berta Lawrence immediately springs to thought, with her passionate invocations of the shire, its history and folklore. Likewise, in the 1920s, we read Mrs A.C. Osborne Hann's lively and extraordinarily engrossing *Somerset*, recollecting the poet Samuel Coleridge's stay at his much-loved Nether Stowey, 'And now, beloved Stowey, I behold thy church tower, and me thinks the four huge elms clustering, which mark the mansion of my friend', and how Somerset's ethereal presences were ever ready to detonate some of his greatest work.

Whereas, formerly it was not the done thing to discuss 'the unexplained', today, spooky subjects are in vogue, and this collection, both baffling and alien to so-called run-of-the-day living, includes never-before published interviews and will hopefully enhance much of Somerset's time-honoured ghost lore.

There is a fine line between the revels of ghosts, folklore and other 'borderline' traditions, therefore a certain amount of overlapping is unavoidable. In fact, the quest for ghosts and ghostly incidents can give, even briefly, insights into their historical setting. Every ghost story is a sign post, clue or link, which may connect us to some other intriguing or enlightening aspect of its time. For example, the spectral soldiers of Sedgemoor might invoke a temptation to examine the implications of that heartbreaking battle, or even lead us to a deeper perspective about the reasons why ghosts are seen at all.

Ghost County

Somerset is 'ghost county'. In the spotlight of modern electricity, we tend to feel safe from anything which purports to be mysterious. Should you decide to step into the world of ghosts, then you would be well advised to be acquainted with at least a passable key to Somerset's otherworldly realms. Explorers of unearthly happenings claim it is one of the most haunted counties in England; a genuine hunting ground for seekers of the unexplained.

Somerset's ghostly legends are a complex weave in which truth and fiction mix and mingle in a medley of oral and written tradition, to be found in early books, pamphlets, periodicals and newspapers. Many tales have been passed down, almost word for word, becoming accepted as part of our supernatural lore. In the late 1900s, the weekly magazine *Tit Bits* stated that the belief in the supernatural was so prevalent throughout the shire, that the paper asked the county's clergy to preach on the subject to warn their parishioners about the dangers of superstition. On 31 July 2006, *The Times* wrote that 'Churchgoers in Britain are still highly superstitious and centuries of preaching the Gospel have failed to banish belief in omens and portents of good and bad luck'. Many of the beliefs, the newspaper said, mentioned actions to ward away ghosts; such as gesturing the sign of the cross, hanging a horseshoe in the porch and using the redemptive power of salt.

J.A. Garton in *Glowing Embers from a Somerset Hearth* (1936) wrote:

> Superstition in still strong in the West Country, and, in these enlightened days, people laugh at the hereditary instinct which has a wholesome respect for the 'Unseen' and for anything which is not understood; yet this instinct may not be so distantly related to that very quality which Faith in the Almighty requires.

A recent Gallup poll reported that one third of those surveyed confirmed their belief in ghosts. Television and radio present regular programmes on the activities of ghost hunters, ghost clubs and other out-of-this-world events. Nearly everyone fancies a good ghost story, especially if it is anchored in supposed fact. And, talking of anchors, there are several frightening accounts of phantom ships and uncanny beaches.

In spite of centuries of change, ghosts have not aged. They move, sway, fade and reappear among us. Scratch a local rumour or legend and there is nearly always someone willing to weave and delve into what, how, or if it happened. Of the myriad interviews and research into bygone pamphlets, news cuttings and other appraisals of spectral encounters, some veils have lifted, whereas others are cloaked by time or lack verifiable detail.

Aside from ghostly figures, places and other images, Somerset is said to be well populated by spirit birds and beasties. The Greek biographer and philosopher Plutarch (*c.* 46–120 AD) abhorred the eating of meat and wondered whether animals may have souls. In one of his essays, he considers reincarnation, where nature transmutes everything '… with different fleshy coats new clothing all' (*Plutarch's Writings,* Vol. 5, trans. William Baxter). Here, there is also a connection, with the ability of witches to shape-shift into other sentient beings, such as hares and foxes. Moreover, earliest records describe sightings of animal and human phantoms. Plutarch continues, 'It is ordained by Fate that every soul, whether with or without understanding, when gone out of the body, should wander for a time, though for all the same, in the region lying between the earth and the moon'. Could these 'wanderers', with their occasional eavesdropping across that finite line between life and afterlife, be an explanation for what we call "ghosts" or "spirits"?

Ghosts are more or less accepted to be 'memory imprints', whereas spirits are believed to be conscious beings from a parallel dimension. Others believe they are one and the same thing. They can be experienced by anyone at any given moment. Mediums and people with what is called the 'sixth sense' find it easier to link with them. Therefore, it seems spiritually logical that every created thing, whether inanimate or animate, is imbued with an invisible aura. In Homer's *Odyssey,* the Ghost of Anticlea says:

> My son, most illfated of all mankind, it is not Proserpine that is beguiling you, but all people are like this when they are dead. The sinews no longer hold the flesh and bones together; these perish in the fierceness of consuming fire as soon as life has left the body, and the soul flits away as though it were a dream.

Talking of flesh and bones, a recent radio programme featured 'ghost limbs' – stating that many people who have an arm, hand or leg amputated, tell of 'feeling' that the limb is still there. The challenge of contemporary ghost analysis is to establish the difference between possible imaginings or other psychological anomalies, and a real haunting.

Years of specialist fieldwork by paranormal science, does outline a growing number of baffling incidents in the same way as ufologists are perplexed by unidentified objects in the heavens. And in Somerset, UFOs have enjoyed their share of media popularity. The art of telling a spooky experience can still ignite a shiver in heart and mind. Even so, there are fewer new yarns, but we shall always be eager to enjoy a retelling of the old ones.

Somerset's own history of the supernatural is exciting and memorable. In mapping the county's ghostly activities, we shall meet almost every known type of unearthly visitation, from vanishing buildings, haunted castles, screams and shrieks, inns, roads and paths, to animals, ships, figures and icy surprises, or to things that literally go 'bump in the night' … or day. Any exhaustive study of Somerset's hauntings would fill volumes, and again, I have attempted to strike a balance between some of our celebrity spectres to the less known, including several contemporary and hitherto unpublished encounters. There are no horizons.

Climate Change – More Ghosts!

The scorching crackle of nature's electricity and the explosive boom of thunder have blazed the background of many spine-chilling films and plays. The weather, albeit stormy, seems to play its own part in many of our creepy tales. Psychic science claims that more ghosts abound during the heightened magnetic field of thunderstorms. Spirits, spooks and other phenomena are believed to be more likely to 'return' in the image of 'photographic negatives' during weather extremes. There are countless records of manifestations during thunder tantrums. Shakespeare's phantoms mostly arrive in a thunderstorm. In this scene from *Macbeth*, Thunder, an apparition of a blood-covered child rises and calls out: 'Macbeth! Macbeth! Macbeth!' Macbeth responds, 'Had I three ears, I'd hear thee'. Again, the haunted battlements of *Hamlet* and Herne the spectral hunter in the *Merry Wives of Windsor,* are but a few of literature's dramatic visitations.

With climate change upon us, some leading meteorologists warn that rising temperatures will be partly responsible for severer electrical storms, which will undoubtedly increase the random appearances of extra-terrestial bugaboos. Over the centuries, Somerset has numerously recorded anomalic-weather visions. *Somerset Notes and Queries (1895)* recorded:

> On Thursday, June 19th, 1662, in the evening, between Upper Compton and Trent, in the County of Somerset, the sky being much clouded and dark, so that it was thought the sun was set, on a sudden the sun began to break forth, but before it came to its brightness, it appeared very fiery and bloody, and the reflection of it upon a town called Bing-weston [not far from Upton Compton], was such, that the spectators thought it had been on fire: after this it shone very clear and bright, and in it was seen a man on horseback very perfectly; in a short space after there appeared another sun, about two yards distance [as that conceived] from the first sun on the north side of it, then immediately appeared very plainly a man on horseback in this other sun: also both these men on horseback for a small space of time stood and faced each other: after that on the west side of the real sun, was seen a great army fixed, but because of the multiplicity of them, it could not be easily discerned whether they were horse or foot: But there was plainly seen another army both of horse and foot coming out of the north and marching very near the northern sun, and there they made a halt for a very short space of time, and then moved again, and marched very swiftly into the northern sun …

This report which continues to describe this ghostly army's movements, ends '… testified by an eye witness'.

Ancient Auras

'They old places hev a-kep they ghosts', said the old countryman in Stogursey's Greyhound Inn. 'Yur'll find plenty round.' Broken dialect, maybe, but it told that he was full of years, and 'knew a thing or two.'

For centuries, the county has been called 'The Isles of the Dead', 'The Blessed Land', 'The Summer Land', even 'God's Country', a lost far away echo of the early Celtic 'Tir tairngiri', or 'Land of Promise', an abode of souls. Pre-Christian interment placed the departed with the head usually facing pagan north, later changed to the Christian east. The northerly compass was anciently revered as the sphere for the near departed.

Somerset's landscape is a trove of burial mounds and prehistoric pilgrim tracks that lead to sacred groves and stone circles. Among the rites for the dead, archaeological finds, implements and oral tradition, tell of elaborate rituals, including those to prevent the individual's spirit, or as the Egyptians called it, the 'Ka', becoming an earthbound ghost, or 'lost soul.' The mysterious names for these venerable areas have largely lost their meaning but some can be traced to some deity, or similar spiritual significance. For whatever cause, myriads of them stay haunted. Interestingly, and for whatever reasons, the locations of many haunted places are ancestral settlements sited near the towns and villages that have developed around them or within close proximity, such as healing pools, wells, tumuli, sacred stones and other pre-historic remnants.

True or not, villagers who protested that a new housing estate would 'harm the fairies' living in their midst have forced a property company to scrap its building plans and start again. Marcus Salter, head of Genesis Properties, estimates that the small colony of fairies believed to live beneath a rock in St Fillans, Perthshire, has cost him £15,000, reported *The Times* on 21 November 2006. The newspaper said that Mr Slater claimed a villager came over shouting, 'Don't move that rock. You'll kill the fairies'. This has echoes of Somerset's numerous faery-haunted areas, where even today the indigenous population is jealously watchful over local earthworks and stone circles.

It is reckoned that if you are looking for life-departed figures, faces, shapes and animals during the dark of the moon, you might at least feel them, or glimpse them as 'blacker than the blackness itself'. Alternatively, your chances of a verifiable appearance are best during moonlit nights. Here are some well-known Somerset possibilities: the Bronze Age barrow near Kingdom Farm, above Cheddar; Castle Cary Earthworks near Park Pond; Williton's Battle Gore Earthworks on the Williton-to-Watchet road; King's Castle behind the golf links; the amphitheatre; Charterhouse; Trendle or Trundle Ring on the exposed hillside, east of and above Bicknoller church; Stantonbury Camp, left of the main Bath to Wells road near Stanton Prior village; Small Down Camp, Evercreech; Cow Castle, Simonsbath; Bury Castle, Selworthy and King Alfred's Fort, Burrowbridge. These are richly suffused with apparitions and unforgettable presences. Take a camera … and maybe a bottle of smelling salts!

Mysterious Bath

A giant stone was heaved into Bath's sparkling springs by Bladud, the son of ancient British King, Hudibras, wrote twelfth-century chronicler Geoffrey of Monmouth. The early historian claimed that it was part of a magical spell to imbue the waters with healing powers. A later version relates how Bladud, as a result of suffering from leprosy, was banished, and wandering far and wide found work as a swineherd at Keynsham. Soon his herd became infected with the disease. Fearing discovery, he led them to the other side of the river, where suddenly the beasts plunged into a quagmire of mud and bubbling springs. Bladud guided them to the river bank but in washing the mud from their skins, he saw that the leprosy had vanished. Bladud bathed in the waters and was also cured. Consequently, he built the baths around the healing waters and a city was born.

'All night long, the ghosts and shades of a forgotten civilisation murmured in the leaves, chuckled in the water, creaked on the stair,' noted the poet and author Dame Edith Sitwell in her compelling 1932 book *Bath*, in which she charts the fame and fortunes of the city's distinguished names, including the swaggering Beau Nash, royal visitors, artists, writers, politicians and poets.

What the illustrious author might have thought of the innumerable sightings of ghosts in the prestigious Theatre Royal and other notable addresses is a matter of opinion, especially that of a tortoiseshell butterfly which occasionally flutters during the pantomime season. This fragile creature was first spotted during a performance of the 1948 Christmas panto. A whimsical edge is given to spirit butterflies in *Somerset & Dorset Notes & Queries* (Vol. 3) from a Somerset villager:

> I find an interesting belief prevailing here, especially I think among the old, that during sleep the soul is often absent from the body, and (strange in a remote Somersetshire village to be reminded of the Myth of the Psyche) that in such cases it frequently assumes the form of a butterfly.
>
> I had a long account from an aged man, which his wife entirely confirmed, of two labouring men who after their *al fresco* dinner sat down beside a pond. One dropped off to sleep, and the other noticed a butterfly flitting over the surface of the water, and at times touching it. Whenever the butterfly touched the water, the sleeping man was observed to start. On waking he said that he had had a fearful dream – that someone had been trying to drown him, and that he was most thankful to awake. That the man's soul was in the butterfly my informants had no doubt. They were also firmly of opinion that the extreme difficulty sometimes experienced in waking was to be ascribed to the fact that the soul was absent, and that it was impossible to rouse the sleeper until such time as she had winged her flight homeward to 'her mansion in this fleshly nook', at any rate that the attempt to do so might be fraught with grave danger to the sleeper.

Dame Edith's delightful *Bath Address Book* includes Admiral Viscount Nelson's address at Pierreport Place, near the Bath Festival office, where a member of staff heard footsteps climbing the stairs. Other invisible sounds, floating figures, dark shapes and curious manifestations occupy many of Bath's exquisite Georgian streets, lanes and buildings, including the Sydney Place residence of Jane Austen, William Pitt, Earl of Chatham at The Circus, and as a child, Sir Walter Scott at South Parade. Could that dashing society worthy Beau Nash have any part of The Garrick's Head hauntings? After all, the hotel was his home, Saint John's Court, before it became The Garrick's Head.

Adjacent to the Theatre Royal, it has an abundance of unusual happenings. During the 1980s a theatre art exhibition promoter said that she had not '… encountered anything ghostly other than unexplained but strong feelings. I'm told that over the years an apparition visits one of the boxes' – along with a fragrance of jasmine – which brings us to the 'Grey Lady'. Her sudden materialisation is well vouched for, says a Theatre Royal web release:

> She is dressed in 18th Century evening dress with feathers in her hair. She has no colour, her whole figure appears as grey. At times she appears solid although sometimes as a wispy, smokey figure.
>
> There are differing accounts as to her origin. The most popular version is that she is the ghost of a lady who killed herself after her husband killed her lover in a duel. The second account is that she fell madly in love with an actor at the theatre and spent all her time watching him from the top box. As her love was unrequited she committed suicide. The third version is the same as the second one except that the roles of the lady and the actor are reversed. Her suicide is agreed in all versions. She hung herself behind a door in the Garrick's Head, the theatre's own pub.
>
> The Grey Lady's favourite haunt in the theatre is the top left hand box facing the stage, although she has also appeared in the opposite box. She has also been seen in the corridor of the Dress Circle. It would seem that she just does a re-run of the same actions.

The actress Dame Anna Neagle, and other members of the 1975 production *The Dame of Sark*, are all said to have seen her. However, a ghostly departure or difference occurred during a conversation with a former Bath author 'A' whose associations with the city's culture have been considerable:

> Grey Lady or not, I have, and I know others who have, seen the figure of a man in and around the stage. He is dressed in 18th century wear, and, if you ask me, he is Henry Irving. The likeness was incredible, and I'm not confusing him with the theatre's 'Phantom Doorman'. You have to remember that Irving was the greatest actor of his time. He was Somerset born.

Irving, who was born at Keinton Mandeville in 1838, started his professional career in Sunderland, then London, and travelled world wide receiving dazzling accolades from the public and critics. William Winters, the famous American critic, summed up his thoughts of Irving, saying 'if the light that shone through his work was not the light of genius, by what name could it be called?' In 1905, following an emotionally charged farewell performance during the theatre's centenary year, Irving took his last bow. He died in Bradford that same year. He is buried in Westminster Abbey. The year 2008 will mark 170 years since his birth.

Floating candles, knockings and tappings, objects moving involuntarily, glowing lights and door handles turning, seem all part and parcel of the Garrick's Head, and a former landlord, Peter Welch, is on record as being in no doubt about its haunted reputation.

Among other of the city's famous ghosts is the 'man in black' or 'the man in a black hat' – a really chilly encounter for some witnesses, or sheer fascination for others. This 'man,' out of the ordinary character, was mentioned in the 1800s, walking between Portland Place and George Street, and several people have made sketches of him which were published in Margaret Royal's *Local Ghosts*. His notoriety grew, especially with his comings and goings in various parts of the assembly rooms, built and furnished in 1769 by seventy trustees, and costing over £20,000. The work of John Wood 'the younger,' these splendid rooms have been at the heart of Bath's cultural and social life in more ways than one; the 'one' must be their own exclusive ghost … with a few extra thrown in for eerie measure!

Descriptions of the black hat vary, and it has been likened to 1800s Quaker-style hat. One lady is quoted as having seen the black-hatted gentleman walking down Saville Row, heading towards the assembly rooms. She said he wore a sweeping black cloak, gaiters and black breeches. Seen in the Assembly Rooms by staff and visitors, the author noted the following comments:

> I know that Gay Street is well spooked, and I suspect that the Man in the Black Hat is among them. Dr Samuel Johnson used to stay there with a lady friend, and her house was often buzzing with voices, and a man with a pony-tail hair bob, tied by a ribbon. Anyway, the Black hatted man gave several people quite a fright many, many years ago in the Card Room. I saw him one early evening standing and watching something on the lawns near the Saville Row side of the building. It's a really strangely beautiful place, this.

Victoria Park's Gravel Walk is where a white-haired man has been seen. A student saw him in daylight, 'A middle-aged man I was talking to started babbling about a transparent white-haired man standing at the top of the steps. He was so affected by what he saw that I called for an ambulance and he was taken to hospital and treated for shock'.

That erstwhile ghost hunter, Peter Underwood, records that in the 1800s the poet laureate William Wordsworth resided at the Grosvenor Hotel. He may have heard this tale, that apparently one early morning, the son of the manageress saw the misty shape of a woman. She disappeared into 'thin air' in what was called the Conference Room.

The George Inn, Bathampton, boasts the returning visits of Jean Baptiste Du Barr'e, who took his final breath there after being taken there following a duel. A number of patrons say he leans on the bar, usually in December.

Behind the medieval wall opposite the Theatre Royal is a considerable down drop. The groans and calls of buried plague victims are heard. The wall was a city boundary during the period of the Great Plague.

The Headless Horseman

Just beyond Cannington, past the King's Head Inn, a lane reaches out to a desolate field encircling a quarry. It is called the Warren. Archaeological excavations may have answered the talk about 'several misty figures' and the area's sometimes sombre mood. Not only were a number of skeletons unearthed, but experts believe it is the site of a huge battle because several of the skeletons showed signs of injury.

Cannington Park's saga has parallels with Windsor Great Park's famous Herne the Hunter, spurring forth a pack of demon hounds on misty mornings. Cannington's Cynwit's Castle, a mile north-west of Cannington village, is said to be very haunted by scary faeries and a demonic wild hunt. Although this wilderness of scrub, rocky outcrops and woodland might not come under the 'no man's land' between Holford and the Castle of Comfort Inn, where a coach and four black horses suddenly thunder from nowhere to sink into the ground near Walford's Gibbet, it nevertheless qualifies as another fright zone.

Cannington Park – eerie noises and unidentifiable shapes.

Cannington Park area where the wild hunt has been heard.

Cannington Park's headless horsemen of 'The Devil's Hunting Ground' have given the Park's wilderness, a grim reputation. It has also given good incentive for the locally superstitious to uphold the custom of either carrying a small cross of aspen wood, wear blue or simply avoid the place after sunset, particularly the south-east fields, marked as a battle with the Danes in AD 878, where over the years, human skeletons and arrowheads have been unearthed.

The Sleeping King

It is believed that there is an invisible door in Cadbury Hill, Nailsea. As part of an oral tradition surrounding the earthwork, whoever finds this door and enters will encounter the ghosts of King Arthur and his Knights of the Round Table. It is one of three camps with that title, the other being at Congresbury ,which is said to be guarded by a white horse.

The most famous is Cadbury Castle at West Camel and Queen Camel. Grassy mounds are believed to be the leftovers of Arthur's palace, and a drove called King Arthur's Hunting Causeway, leads to Glastonbury Tor. An oral tradition, some of which was recorded by the late Revd E. Skelton and a local gardener, between 1906–29, attempts to reinforce the legend that Cadbury Castle is the King's authentic palace. It is on record that Arthur and his knights have been seen riding round the ramparts.

Glastonbury Tor is steeped in legends of King Arthur and otherworldly events.

The claim that Cadbury is the genuine Camelot, along with its ghostly aura, is mentioned by historian M.A. Rowland:

All writers tell of the legend that prevails to our present times that Arthur and his Knights sleep under the great hill. The belief was prevalent in Leland's time (1540), and in 1902, when a student from Wells was told by an artist and antiquarian that on visiting South Cadbury an old native of the place asked him, 'Have you come to take the King out?' The King and his Knights are said to ride out in the moonlight and that the horses are shod with silver; a silver horseshoe has been found there.

The argument that Arthur was buried in Cornwall was raised by a correspondent to *Somerset & Dorset Notes & Queries* (Vol.1.VIII. 1889):

A strange story came to my ears last August, and as my informant was a man to whose word no exception can be taken, there seems little doubt of its authenticity. An Antiquary, for the present I will call him A, was rambling near Camelford in Cornwall, and falling into conversation with an old man learnt, very much to his surprise, that he was close to the grave of King Arthur. The old fellow, annoyed at the statement that the King (if he ever existed) was interred at Glastonbury Abbey, challenged our Antiquary to examine a kind of recess in the bank of the

Atmospheric Glastonbury Abbey.

little River Camel. Divesting himself of boots and socks, A – waded to the spot indicated, and there, sure enough, *was* a hollow about seven feet in length. Within was a slab – how placed I cannot say – and on it this inscription: *Hic jacet Arturus Rex.* The Cornishman could afford no information, and A – departed in a state of some bewilderment.

Whether this eternal King factually belonged to Somerset is still controversial, as other claimants include Wales, Scotland and Cornwall. Some say that he came from Yorkshire. Even so, Somerset has the most prolific trove of Arthurian legends attended by a large retinue of spectral appearances. Recounting an experience near Glastonbury Abbey in 1930, Lord Darling wrote:

… as I descended the slope of a barren hillock, I observed a man who bore little resemblance to the ordinary dwellers in those parts. His dress was altogether that of an earlier age, though he himself seemed hardly beyond middle life. Attired somewhat in the fashion of a shepherd in the days when shepherds and poets were more alike … 'You study to find the hidden springs, Sir?' said I, when we had journeyed a short distance together. 'Ay, Sir,' he replied, 'Springs – of which there be many kinds – and waves, of which I have learned more, for should not each of us try – as I have heard Lord Bacon advise – to take all learning for his province?'

'Truly so, Sir', I said, 'had we his industry or his capacity. But surely I was mistaken in supposing you to mean that you had heard those words spoken by Lord Bacon himself?'

'No, Sir, indeed you err not', he replied, 'and he might positively give you yourself the same assurance could I tarry here awhile – but already my lengthening shadow tells me that I am somewhat overdue elsewhere – 'on the skirts of Bagley Wood, where most the Gipsies by the turf-edged way pitched their smoked tents'. So saying, he stepped out of the moonlight into the shadow cast by the cloister wall, and was lost to sight.

Here is another graphic reminder of Arthur's returning spirit. It was written by one of Somerset's foremost writers, the late Berta Lawrence in her *Somerset Legends*:

On Christmas Eve the ghostly company rides out of the camp and descends in another direction to the village of Sutton Montis below Cadbury, moving more slowly and sedately, for the slope is precipitous. They ride along the quiet road towards Sutton Montis church and let their horses drink from the stone-rimmed well that is now inside the orchard of Abbey House, really a medieval priest's house of Ham stone. People in Sutton Montis, including some who say they are not superstitious, have heard the chink of hooves, the ghostly jingle of a bridle, on some Christmas Eve when they lay awake, As the well is inside the orchard and now covered, the drinking place could be the clear little runnel of water that issues between fronds of hart's tongue fern from a bank in the lane ... On nights of the full moon the horsemen ride round the ramparts and their horses' shoes flash silver ... A true hearted person who bathed his eyes in the well might see the hill open, and glimpse Arthur and his men sleeping a tranced sleep within, swords near at hand ready for the day when Arthur comes again.

Porlock: Weir and Hill

Hill climbers and ramblers often report strange and 'distant voices', and on occasions feel as if 'being watched' by unseen eyes in and around Porlock's Berry Castle, situated on a lower ride of one of Exmoor's combes, acclaimed for its scenic beauty. This points us to the enchanting little town, lovely Porlock Weir, and its quaintly recently established festival of the arts and literature.

Spectres, coffins, baying hounds are part and package of Porlock Hill's Pandora's box of brooding events. Another problem is that some of the legends have become distorted in the re-telling. Nevertheless, one of the most seasoned tales concerns the hearse 'from nowhere', and a coach and horses speeding out of control. Local folk put many fatal accidents down to the hill's one-in-seven gradient.

Two Sedgemoor battle rebels were hung on Porlock Hill, and they are believed to have been heard 'calling out'. Then there is the account of a stone worker, who cycling over the hill saw a woman wearing a white gown, made bright in the moonlight. Another local man recounted a similar encounter. He even bade the woman 'good evening', when suddenly, she evaporated.

Sea-washed, honey-suckled Porlock and its charming weir are immortalised by the poet Robert Southey, as he sat inspired through the windows of the more than a century-old Old Ship Inn:

Porlock, thy verdant vale so fair to sight,
Thy lofty hills which fern and furze embrown,
The waters that roll musically down ...

Owing to centuries of land change, the weir is two miles from the sea. As with so many coastal habitats, it has its own cultural ethos, including the possibility that it was the seat of one of the

Porlock Weir's haunted steps.

Saxon kings. It has a number of ghosts. A former clairvoyant, Leslie Greenfield, who lived near the church told of the figure of a man seen by the steps. The echoing of horses has also been reported over the years.

Curdon's Pixy Spirits

The pretty little hillside village of Stogumber boasts one of the hardest to find and reach promontory fortresses, Curdon Camp, carpeted with undergrowth and thick foliage. It is in Curdon Copse, which locals say is haunted by 'queer looking pixies', and will-o-the-wisps have been witnessed hovering over its brook.

Roman Soldiers

Hamdon Hill is rich in ghost lore and is among Somerset's most mythically topical talking points. Its fortifications silhouette a noble grandeur seen from its eastern entrenchments from the Yeovil-Ilminster road; itself a highly haunted highway. Described as more settlement than camp, its fortified domain extends over three miles in circumference, being used since Neolithic times by early man, Celts and Romans. A huge collection of unearthed discoveries may be seen in Taunton Castle Museum: Roman coins from the eastern boundary, skeletons in the northerly

An ancient copse – reputedly the haunt of pixies.

compass, and other coins, bronze shovels and flint axes in other quarried areas. Hamdon Hill is, as some might say, 'seriously haunted', with descriptions of 'bizarre shapes outlined by light', to those of Roman soldiers walking the hilly ramparts.

With over forty years of journalism to his pen, eventually becoming the editor of Somerset's *Western Gazette,* the late G.F. Munford was an avid collector of supernatural tales. Several of these appeared in 1922 titled *Ghosts and Legends of South Somerset.* One of his favourites, which he wrote as a colourful romance, concerned a local witch whose spirit is still said to haunt the district. And another startling story tells of a motorist, Mr David G., who told a friend not to disclose any of the following details until after his death, which occurred in 1958, '… because I think people will think I'm mad', he said, adding, 'You can make of it whatever, but I know what I saw'.

David G., a retired postal worker, was visiting friends in a nearby hamlet of Hamdon Hill. It was a humid afternoon in the summer of 1957 and his first excursion to Somerset. He was driving along the boundary of the hill, not far from the fort, which he could see from the road:

There wasn't another car in sight, and though it was broad daylight, I couldn't help feel that something wasn't right. I was also feeling tired, but not sleepy. There were lots of people walking towards me. Bit of a surprise. I stopped and turned off the engine. The shock of it was that these people were dressed in armoured uniforms. They looked the spitting image of Roman soldiers, bit like the ones I had seen in *The Robe,* which was showing that year in town.

I really thought a film was being shot, until they just kept coming on and walked right through the car and me. Everything turned very cold. Believe me, it took me a long time to get started. I arrived to my friends safe and sound. Never said a word, until you brought up the subject of ghosts.

There are those who claim to be able to 'see', 'sense' or 'hear' ghostly occurrences. And there is a huge interest in 'things unknown', which attracts thousands of visitors to haunted areas, and even involve themselves in ghost tours, clubs and research groups, many of which have their own newsletters and networking links. Since the advent of photography and sound recording, there are others who claim to have photographed and made sound recordings of supernatural visitors. There are said to be almost countless faery hauntings, which believers say always begin with the rapid movements of gleaming globes of light. Similarly, certain psychic phenomena is allied with orbs or streaks of light, and recently, the Somerset ghost researcher Ian Gibson-Small pointed to a series of photographs showing these unusual light formations in photographs taken in a local property.

Faery Fair and Crowcombe Devilry

Interestingly, many people from all paths of life, some of them so-called nonbelievers, have admitted to seeing ghostly activities. One hair-raising anecdote was retold in 2005 to a correspondent of *The Somerset Reviewer*:

> We shall call him Tim. The meeting was at The Blue Ball inn, at Triscombe, below the long beech lined walk over the Quantocks. Tim was in his teens when it happened: 'Everyone who knows me knows that I never believed in ghosts or whatever', he said. 'I think I saw the ghosts of faeries, or something like it'.
>
> Following our lunch, Tim led me along the heavily wooded track, until we reached a dip, which opened out into a small glade, surrounded by ferns and mossy banks. I was on the way to the pub. It wasn't dark. My eye caught some lights, sort of tiny but loads of them. I could make out small human-like figures and what I thought to be stalls and swings. There was music. Then it all faded. I tell you, I had a damn good drink that night … and I went home with friends in a car. I've never done the walk again, except for now, to show you.

For many years, the nearby village of Crowcombe has gathered quite an archive of superstitions, witchcraft and untoward incidents. In fact, both the village and its environs are well dunked with folk belief and magical traditions. It was also the focus for one of England's most noted folklorists, the late Ruth Tongue, whose collection of folk tales, songs and folk magic continues to be an invaluable source of information. A close friend of Ruth's, who has recently died, privileged me with numerous unpublished material, and many hours were shared listening and discussing Somerset's folk customs and Miss Tongue's fascinating interests:

> I kept a little shop there for a while, and Ruth and I used to banter and exchange all sorts of snippets about this witch, that ghost or some of the old herbal remedies and even folk songs that still haven't seen the light of day. Many times I would visit her old cottage where she shared her space with all kinds of animals and birds. She really did have a magical touch with wildlife.

Crowcombe Parish church – said to have been attacked by the devil.

Crowcombe resembles a village in a large dell set below high hills, painted in blue heathers, with ancient barrows, woodlands and streams. The fourteenth-century parish church and its opposite Church House are allegedly haunted by all kinds of faintly silhouetted characters.

One of the most dramatic events was claimed to have been a visit by 'Satan himself'. There are other versions, among which certain members of the church believe that a number of ghosts appeared 'when the Devil himself attacked the spire'. *The Postmaster* newspaper of 8 January 1725 detailed the following vivid report:

> We have the following remarkable account from Crowcombe in Somersetshire: That on Sunday the 20th post, between Two and Three of the Clock in the Afternoon, whilst the bell was summoning the Parishioners to Divine Service, and not a few of the Congregation waited the Revd. Minister's Coming, some being seated in the church, and others in the church Porch: a very terrible Lightning, attended with a most frightful clap of Thunder (more loud than a Peal of Ordnance), attacked the said Building. It appeared to the exterior Spectators as if a vast number of Fire-Balls were shot against the Steeple; which was shock'd and split in such a strange manner, that the light now penetrates thro' the Crevices between the Stones in every Square of Panel. A large stone, of 200lb Weight, from between the battlements of the Tower and the Steeple, was forcibly lifted over the battlements … and thrown into the churchyard … the Great Bell, which itself was then tolling, was broken in Pieces …

The long and detailed news item continues in great detail about the widespread damage to the building. Many members of the congregation were also struck down by the lightning, but later recovered. The Devil, ghosts or otherwise, the amount of destruction still lives in the memory of local people.

Part of Crowcombe's Elizabethan Rectory is favoured by the 'Blue Lady,' said only to appear to children. Sightings of her are rare. Attired entirely in blue, with matching blue shoes, she was last seen in 1929. There are various theories as to her identity, and it has been assumed that she may be a member of the Carew family, whose ancient ancestry is rooted in nearby Crowcombe Court.

Mother Leakey

Once one of West Somerset's most prestigious resorts, especially favoured during its Victorian heyday, Minehead is much a shadow of its former glories, yet retains many amiable reminders of fine gardens and cosy retreats. Nestled between hill, vale and the Severn Sea, it formed part of the nearby pre-Norman Manor of Porlock, held by Algar, Earl of Mercia.

The little town's claim to ghostly goings-on, is overshadowed by the ghost of Mother Leakey. Reportedly, Mrs Leakey, who can unexpectedly appear at any given moment, was a witch, capable of storm raising and sinking ships. She has been blamed for the sinking of *The Lamb*

Mother Leakey's parlour symbolises Minehead's ghostly legend.

on 28 February 1736, reported in *Read's Weekly Journal*. Here is an updated and edited excerpt. concerning Leakey from the *State Papers Domestic, Charles I*, Vol. 383, No 5, 'The Examination of the business concerning the reported Apparition at Minehead in the County of Somerset'. Leakey devotees believe this sheds a more reliable light, than numerous later and fantastical versions:

This Examinate (witness) says that her Mother-in-Law said (lying upon her death-bed in her house) she would come again after her death. To whom she replied, 'what will you be a devil?' 'No but I will come in the Devil's likeness'.

And said that her Mother-in-law made her Will and left her husband some household stuff which she had to the value of twenty pounds, and a bond of twenty pounds due from Dr. Atherton, and a bond of twenty pounds due from William Leakey, of Barnstaple deceased before her; and further she said that about six weeks after her death, there was a knocking and noise in the chamber, and about the bed, which went away like a drove of cattle; and further said, that about a twelve-month after old Mother Leakey's death, John Leakey, of the age of fourteen years, grandchild to old Widow Leakey, and living in the said Alexanders house, died of a languishing disease, and that in the time of his sickness, he complained that he could not be quiet, for his grandmother, but he did not tell her that he saw his grandmother, and that when he died he cried out that he saw the Devil, and that there was no print of a hand to be seen about the throat of the child after his death, but somewhat black about the neck (as some said they saw him).

In all this time which was a year and two months she saw no apparition, and further she said that the first time her mother appeared to her was three weeks before Easter, and that going into her chamber to bed with a book in her hand she saw within her chamber, sitting in a chair, her mother in her full proportion, and in her usual apparel, and being much astonished she beheld it a quarter of an hour but could not speak to it nor stir, and at last, it vanished away with a mighty groan, which the maid below in the kitchen hearing came up and asked her mistress what she ailed.

A Luccombe parson, Dr Henry Byam, was also called 'to give her rest'. Minehead residents told him that she haunted local streets, the beach and fields 'whistling' and generally making other noises. Dr. Byam is recorded as believing that during her life, Mother Leakey, contrary to the tittle-tattle of her practising witchcraft, was a Christian, and a popular and friendly soul. She was buried at Minehead's St Michael's church on 5 November 1634.

The inquiry's clerk, a Mr Heathfield, also offered spiritual protection against the spirit. The upshot of various investigations and offers of religious help did not seem to 'lay' Mrs Leakey, as over the passage of time, reports of her sudden appearances have not abated.

Grave Tidings

The shrieking, shrouded ghost of Lady Florence Wyndham of Watchet's Kentisford manorial farm, is redolent of the classic British Hammer Horror film genre. There are so many versions about the Watchet White Lady, or Lady Wyndham's Ghost, that you can take your pick. The author, who lives in Watchet and has had long associations with the Wyndham saga, via his talks with the late Katherine Wyndham and older inhabitants familiar with the 'passed down' accounts, believes that the C.H. Poole version, penned in the 1800s, is probably one of the more terrifying descriptions:

The Wyndham plaque – marks the last resting place of Florence Wyndham.

… the mother of Sir John Wyndham, who, being supposed dead, was buried alive in the vaults of St. Decuman's. Happily for her, the sexton, hearing some noise, as he shut the door, was attracted by it. Listening, he discovered whence the sound came. Opened the coffin, and to his utter astonishment beheld the lady alive.

What happened after that has become a point of speculation and fantasy. In 1872, the *Cornhill* magazine reported that a local schoolmaster confided to a group of thieves that Lady Florence Wyndham had been interred along with 'seven rings of gold studded with precious stones'. With threats, they forced him to accompany them to the vault:

The schoolmaster lifted up the coffin-lid, and began taking the rings off the dead woman's hands. Six of them he got off easily, but the seventh he couldn't manage. She had doubled up her finger, and wouldn't let the ring go. The robbers threw him a knife, 'Cut off her finger, then!', one growled … but the moment he cut off the finger – that very moment the dead woman awoke, as if from sleep, and cried aloud with a terrible voice – 'Brothers and sisters! Arise quickly and help me! No rest had I during my life, and now will they let me have none, even immediately after death!'

At the sound of her voice the coffins burst open, and the Dead began to come forth. The robbers heard the noise they made, and fled; the terrified schoolmaster ran up the staircase leading from the crypt, rushed into the church, hid himself in the choir, and slammed the door to.

After him rushed the Dead. Seeing where he had hidden himself, they began dragging up their coffins and piling them one on top of another, so as to be able by their help to climb over into the choir. Meanwhile, the schoolmaster, who had found a long pole, began pulling the coffins down with it. In this sort of work he spent the time till midnight. But when

Is the White Lady seen rushing along this path from St Decuman's church the ghost of Lady Wyndham?

twelve o'clock struck – the Dead took down their coffins and went back into the crypt. The schoolmaster was left more dead than alive. Next day he was found in the church terribly ill, an utterly broken man. The priest came, heard his confession, and gave him the Sacrament. Soon after that the schoolmaster expired.

However, many 'Watchetites' believe the following version to have a closer ring of truth. Imagine that time has just chimed fourteen years before 1562; where in Bristol's thriving port Sebastian Cabot has returned to cheering crowds on his sailing adventures in his quest to discover a route to Cathay. And eleven years on, Elizabeth I was making a royal tour of the West Country. Sandwiched between these brief clusters of years, 1562 marked the death of Lady Florence, who had only been married to Sir John Wyndham for barely two years. Lady Florence was pronounced dead after lapsing into a coma during an illness. She was laid to rest in the family vault in St Peter's chapel, St Decuman's Parish church.

It is alleged that a man called Attewell, the sexton, knew that she was wearing valuable rings. Holding aloft a lantern, he went to work, slowly, stealthily, opening the vault. In a struggle to sever one of her gem-bearing fingers, the 'dead' Florence, suddenly sat up screaming for help. Worse, clad only in her shroud, she staggered out of her coffin, seized the sexton's fallen lantern, and fled down the track, over the little pack-horse bridge, crossing the Washford River, and fled home to the farm.

Although deeply shocked by his wife's macabre return from the 'dead', Sir John was overjoyed. Surviving her ordeal of being literally buried alive, Lady Florence was to enjoy a further thirty-four years of life. And the infamous sexton? Needless to say, Attewell, confronted by a 'living corpse', ran terror stricken down St Decuman's hill, leapt into the harbour and was drowned. A descendent of the Attewell family line still lives in the area today.

Nowadays, the ghost of Lady Wyndham still materialises, either motionless, sometimes 'drifting' near the church porch, or is heard and seen screaming as she rushes down the track towards St Decuman's Well, where another legend tells of the saintly missionary St Decuman, who is said to have arrived from Wales to spread the 'Word of the Lord', but was attacked by a local pagan who cut off his head. The ghost of the saint, head under arm, is supposed to haunt the well.

Off The Rails

Downslope from St Decuman's Well, the regular plumes of smoke flurry past as the West Somerset Railway's steam engine chugs its coastal track, offering miles of rural splendour for tourist and local alike. However, uncannily, there is another train that tramps the line. A ghost train!

A tragic accident in 1857 is archived by the then West Somerset Mineral Line Railway, when two trains carrying around thirty labourers collided head on near Kentisford. Three men were killed, and several injured. Ever since, there have been reports of the sound of the accident. Some witnesses claim to have seen one of the trains appear and then vanish. The most recent report of its return was in 1998 when a local man was walking his dog along the Kentisford stretch of track.

Lost Children

Five years ago, the author was shown a walled-up part in an upstairs room at Watchet's Bell Inn. One account gives that the still-born children of a wealthy local family are interred behind the plasterwork and that their spirits haunt the pub. Who knows?

Also, more than one local resident has gone on record about 'being followed' by an invisible presence at the corner where Swain Street meets West Street and the harbour slipway.

Port Sails

One chilling oral tale concerns the sightings of a spectral galleon, told to the writer by an elderly occupant of Almyr Terrace, 'So ee's not seen port sails. Well, durst depend on the weather'. Apparently, the vessel is faintly imaged at certain times, when a heavy sea mist veils the harbour. The elderly person said:

> If a boat puts out to shore, yur'll hear of a death in a three. That's why it's called port sails … the shrouds, yur see!
>
> You telling me about seeing a man in a cloak in the mist, wal I know a gentleman whose blood curdled on The Esplanade, an he warn't soused either. He blinked but could not shift it – the great sail ship. Just there, waiting in the mist, off the right of the mouth … course, ships came in with trade and there's many a tale of smuggling, pirates and the like. An this gentleman's no liar.

Mythical or not, the 'man in a cloak' was said to have been an old 'sea salt' visiting his mistress. Tucked away in the red brick walled entrance is a carving of a sailing vessel, and wedged in an adjoining crack, a coin, symbolising good luck or a specific wish.

Right: *Watchet Harbour today. A ghostly galleon is alleged to appear on misty nights beyond the seaward entrance.*

Below: *Ship carved on a brick.*

Rose Cottage

Tucked in a niche of the ancient port's Esplanade Lane is the quaintly attractive Rose Cottage. However, behind its charming innocence lies the rumours of 'friendly haunters' – footsteps on the stairs and, according to a local ghost researcher, the phantom apparition of a smuggler or perhaps a previous occupant from its early days of 1570 when it was a portreeve cottage, making the owners responsible for collecting taxes at the port and presiding at Watchet's Court Leet. It was recently the home of local business woman Jenny Jones, who writing about the historic dwelling in *The Quantocks Magazine* (2001) said:

> There have been persistent rumours over the years that a secret passage runs under the building. It is said to be one of Watchet's most haunted cottages. I have never been frightened, because I personally haven't ever seen anything. Obviously there are things that cannot be explained, such as stories of residents seeing ghosts. With such a history, and with so many different people living here, there are bound to be tales. For example there were folk living here during the Great Plague of 1646, then yarns about smugglers – and the evacuees of the 40s.

Gallery Ghost

When Nick and Lynda Cotton purchased their now famous art gallery in Swain Street, little did they expect its previous owner would haunt the spacious show rooms! Staunch Methodist Walter Foy opened the shop in 1910, trading as a jeweller and watchmaker. Nick Cotton revealed the rest of the story:

> I can sometimes sense him and occasionally hear the floorboards creak as he paces the space behind where his display counter stood. Then he stops and warms himself by the iron fireplace, which as you can see, still remains. Those who remember him say he liked to keep the fire well-stoked. It is easy to enter a time-slip, because more than once I've suddenly become aware it's a gas-lit shop, and glimpsed the shelves of gleaming jewels and trinklets.

The Raucous Skull

There is a much publicised 'screaming skull', but according to some ear witnesses, it doesn't scream. However, it is said to make unpleasant noises. The skull, still preserved in a locked box in a Chilton Cantelo farmhouse, is believed to be that of Theophilus Brome. In the 1920s, writer John Reed transcribed a manuscript account of Brome's head:

> … it seems to have been preserved at Higher farm since 1829. The title is on the outside of a stiff cardboard cover, consisting of two leaves with a tape fastening. The back page of the cover bears a printed advertisement of *Dr Rees's New Cyclopaedia,* with fine engravings. It may be added that the skull of Theophilus Brome is still preserved in a locked black box in the farm house.

The esteemed *Collinson's History of Somerset, 1791* (Vol. 2, page 339):

A similar skull to that at Chilton Cantelo.

There is a Tradition in this Parish that the person here interred requested that his head might be taken off before his Burial and be preserved at the farm house near the church, where a head, chop-fallen enough, is still shewn, which the Tenants of the house have often endeavoured to commit to the Bowels of the Earth, but have been as often deterred by the horrid noises, portentive of sad displeasure; and about twenty years since (which was perhaps the last attempt) the Sexton, in digging the place for the Skull's repository, broke the Spade in two pieces, and uttered a solemn asseveration never more to attempt an act so evidently repugnant to the quiet of Brome's Head.

Brome, a Midlands man, who died in 1670, instructed that his head be severed before his burial. The story goes that Brome was a plotter against Charles I, beheaded for his defence of the monarchy. The corpses of known regicides were exhumed and their heads cut off and displayed in public places as a means of posthumous punishment. To pre-empt such a fate, Brome had his head removed. Over fifty years ago, Brome's tomb in the north transept of St James' church in Chilton Cantelo was opened. A headless skeleton was found.

The late Peter Underwood, president of the Ghost Club Society was shown the skull by the then owner of the farm. The reburial of the head by successive owners resulted in 'horrid noises'. Brome, it seemed, disliked being disturbed. Underwood wrote, 'The skull is usually kept in a cabinet specially made for it … where it has been for over two hundred years …' Several past owners of the farmhouse have reported noises like a 'rattle' coming from the box. Others claimed it screamed at certain times, but this has been doubted.

Cleeve Abbey Gate House. Ghostly monks and other figures have been seen in the abbey.

Holy Ghosts

Bristol's St Anne's Well at St Anne's Wood, still boasts a ghostly monk, from centuries ago, whose figure holds aloft a bowl of the well's medicinal water. Bare-footed, girdled monks are said to appear at twilight and glide through the walls of Woodspring Priory, near Weston-super-Mare. This sturdy property has been kept in good shape since the dissolution of the monasteries in the reign of Henry VIII.

Haunted by a tall man wearing what some have described as 'animal skin', the long-forgotten, weed-covered healing well of St Pancras is near Cleeve's historic Cistercian Chapel, where monks have been heard chanting ethereal prayers in the meditational stillness. Unearthly monks, including one who counts coins, have been glimpsed among the crumbling walls of Glastonbury Abbey, England's first monastery. The town and its great tor are steeped in memories, including

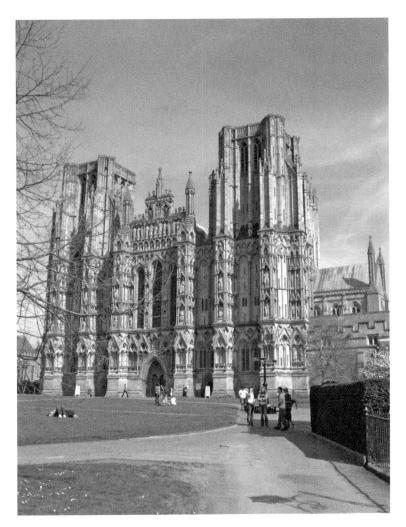

Wells Cathedral where a visitor was spoken to by an invisible presence.

its forgotten legendary buried treasure. Similarly, shadowy shapes have been spotted three miles away at Meare's centuries-old Fish House.

Bruton's Pat Well is said to possess a 'spirit guardian'. Whatever it is, numerous visitors have reported seeing and feeling 'something' that haunts its surroundings. The well is dedicated to St Patrick.

Cathedral Souls

The ornamental grace of Wells Cathedral in England's smallest medieval city of Wells, has been a focus for worship for over 500 years. The imposing, light and airy interior mirrors arches and pillars of sublime architectural proportions. Some visitors have claimed to have been joined by more than one semi-invisible form as they watched and waited for the various performances of the famous clock.

Wells Cathedral Chapter House. A photograph is said to have revealed two figures on the steps.

Is the monk, occasionally spotted in that area, that of Peter Lightfoot? He made the clock in 1325 and is celebrated for the four horse riding knights, who revolve and joust one another as the hour is struck. The clock also shows planetary movements and the phases of the moon.

An American, sightseeing the fourteenth-century choir area, told how, while studying the exquisite Jesse Window, she heard a voice. 'It was almost like a whisper', she remarked to her companion, the artist Michael Roy. Although barely audible, she heard the words, 'I am gladdened'. But no one was there. In 1954, there was a much publicised photograph taken on some steps at the Cathedral Chapter House. Two misty white figures are shown together!

Castle in The Mist

Dunster Castle's dreaming turrets can be seen for miles, and it is one of the National Trust's most popular heritage gems. Seen from the road to Minehead, its big buttressed walls reveal a magical picture, especially when the marsh and sea mists veil its surrounding park and woodland, embodying the very essence of what tourists and explorers expect as the overall image of most European knightly strongholds. It has also left us with an evocative legacy of hauntings. In January 2007, the *Somerset County Gazette* reported:

Dunster Castle in twilight. One of England's most haunted castles.

Ghosts at Dunster Castle will be the subject of a new exhibition this year, owners the National Trust said.

A spokesman said, 'With more than 1,000 years of history, including a civil war siege, it is widely believed that past characters still likely to visit the castle from time to time. In 2007, some of the most popular stories linked to the castle will form the basis of an exhibition and new family trails will allow visitors to discover more about previous inhabitants and explore the castle's darker side'.

Interviewing castle guide June Copp was fascinating. This lively lady is very knowledgeable about its history; more so, the ancient fortification's other 'residents' … the ghosts. As a child, June grew up in the medieval village and her late father was a gardener to the Luttrell family, whose long association with the castle hails to the sovereignty of Edward III.

Dunster Castle's ghost tours have become a major and regular attraction. Before we return to June's interesting anecdotes, it is worth taking a momentary look behind the castle's enduring outlook.

Time's hour glass fills and empties with tales of spirits and unearthly events. Dunster is rated among the UK's most haunted castles, especially for the variety and strangeness of its ghosts' abrupt arrivals. It would seem that from reported sightings, 'things' have also been seen in the areas of the Norman castle's earliest settlements. On the other hand, hauntings are not uncommon at prehistoric or early vicinities of human habitation. Many unexplained descriptions of forms and figures have been recalled at Dunster Deer Park's Bat's Castle, a circular hill encampment high above Dunster Castle.

June Copp said that 'the shop and stables date to the seventeenth century, and this area seems especially prone to supernatural happenings'. June gestured to the twilight area where once sturdy horses were housed. She said:

> A previous shop manager told of a man dressed in green that passed the door of the shop and proceeded down the stable block only to disappear without trace. The next shop manager told of a mysterious green light that floated from the front door to the far end of the stable block, also there was a presence felt by the manager when working in the stock room opposite the shop. She always felt most uncomfortable when working in there. And an assistant manager felt uneasy when unlocking the door between the two sections of the stables and for some reason she always dropped her keys when she unlocked the door.

Over the years, several visitors have remarked of feeling edgy. It is thought that two or three people had been murdered in the stables. Another visitor said that he saw a man in the far left corner of the shop, and assuming it was a gift browser, made to give way, he vanished. He wore a tight-fitting grey jerkin and a loose rag scarf around his neck.

June Copp in front of the room where some members of staff say they have felt a presence.

Dunster Castle's haunted stables.

The famous King Charles' Room, where Charles II is reputed to have slept, has a secret passage. Many people, including castle staff, have heard 'mutterings' in the Leather Gallery, believed to be the voices of cavaliers from the English Civil War, when the castle was besieged. Another 'disturbed' area is the Bell Chamber. A patrolling night watchman took fright on hearing the sound of footsteps. On another occasion, a workman, employed to carry out repairs, said how alarmed he grew at the overwhelming experience that someone was accompanying him up Inner Hall's spiral staircase. His dog refused to move, its hairs proverbially 'standing on end'. Among the castle's most famous ghosts is the Grey Lady, often seen drifting down the seventeenth-century oak staircase, adjacent to the leather gallery.

Walking the Upper Ward, particularly along the battlements, the view gives a panorama of variegated green woodlands, undulating vales, the distinctive Dunkery Beacon, and at one point, the Severn Sea. Dowsers, ley-line hunters and the psychically inclined attribute much of the castle's 'otherworld feel' to its foundation on a Tor. As Draper versed it:

Bold, rising on an insulated height,
With deep, encircling walls, all verdant, crowned,
Thy Castle, Dunster! Proudly meets our sight

Above: *The imposing entrance to Dunster Castle where some visitors have felt they were being 'watched'.*

Left: *Dunster Castle dungeon. Grisly secrets are buried below the floor.*

Nearby the imposing, perpendicular main gate, the oldest part of its bulwark guards a malevolent memory; the dark, dank and claustrophobic dungeon. It was here that captive enemies, thieves, murderers and other offenders were locked up pending trial. Some were never to see freedom again, either dying from ill treatment or disease ... perhaps even the plague because during the 1600s Great Plague, several soldiers, billeted at Dunster, are believed to have succumbed.

June Copp led the way, up steep steps to enter the heavy-walled Dungeon's brooding aura. Few folks, having spent even the briefest moments in this, have denied that 'something' haunts its melancholy mood. That 'something', as June pointed to the floor, could come from its extra occupants because 'below here, are a group of skeletons. When they were discovered some years ago now, it was decided to seal them over. But they are still down there', she said. One of them is a 7-ft male, still manacled in chains! Possibly the remains of the 'giant' are the result of the castle's darker period, under the cruel authority of one of its earliest rulers, William de Mohun, whose reputation for sadistic and bloodthirsty acts are well attested.

So-called giants, or tall and strong men attacking local communities, prevail throughout Somerset. In *Exmoor Wanderings*, Eric R. Delderfield noted:

> During the Civil War the ramp in front of the Castle was filled in, and it was some two hundred years later that Mr George Luttrell decided to excavate it and bring the approaches back to what they are today.
>
> As the work proceeded the thirteenth century gates and a chamber were uncovered, and the skeleton of a man seven feet in height was brought to light. Everything pointed to the fact that the poor wretch had been buried alive. It is one of history's well kept secrets, for nothing more is known as to who he was, or why he had been done to death in such a manner. Other skeletons were discovered nearby. The astounding fact is that the late Mr G.E. Luttrell used to say that every good gun dog he had would always stop in his tracks and make a wagging exploration at the very point where this gruesome discovery was made.

Revisiting the Stable Block, June recalled a dramatic reminder of what can often happen to nonbelievers:

> Some years ago there was a private ghost tour, arranged for a small group of office workers from Taunton. The group consisted of several sceptics, made bolder by having had a few drinks before arriving at the castle. They were standing about half-way down the stable block and the chaps were laughing and joking and making ghostly noises. Suddenly, without warning, a piece of masonry flew down from the ceiling and landed just inside the end stall.
>
> There was a pause in the mirth, but a few seconds later, another piece of masonry came flying down from the same corner of the ceiling. Even the sceptics in the group were now decidedly unsettled and were glad to leave the stables.

An article by Nichola Jones in *The Western Daily Press* (29 March 2007) reports on the activities of a 'new ghost on the block':

> ... apparently a more modern apparition now haunts the corridors and chambers. Property manager William Wake believes the ghost is of a long departed volunteer who still likes to give guests an impromptu tour of her beloved hilltop fortress: 'We get lots of sightings every year', said Mr Wake who has worked at the National Trust property near Minehead, for nine years. 'She was a lovely lady who worked with us here for many years. She used to work in the same

room and was always very highly regarded by the rest of the staff. She eventually retired and later passed away. After that, we had visitors coming to us and complimenting an older lady volunteer. They said she was very helpful and told them all about the room'.

On hearing positive comments from the public, Mr Wake would go to congratulate the guide, only to find all was not what it seemed. The room would be empty or occupied by a male guide. The woman was nowhere to be seen He said: 'We can only assume it's our old volunteer who pops in every now and again to chat to the visitors.

Royal Chop

Although the river Frome divides Somerset and Wiltshire, Farleigh Castle is much a part of Frome. The manor, purchased in 1369 by Sir Thomas Hungerford was transformed into a castle. It is here that a veiled or white lady may be encountered in the chapel. She is thought to be Margaret Plantagenet. Accused by Henry VIII of high treason, she was executed in 1541. According to the telling, she refused to lay her head on the block and attempted to flee. The executioner gave chase, chopping at her whenever he caught up until finally he managed to strike her head from her shoulders.

The Mendips

The author Mrs A.C. Osborne Hann in 1927 said:

I have met people who have told me that in the loneliness of Mendip they have half expected to see some dim and ghoulish figure suddenly emerge, some weird grey devil unexpectedly appear. They refer to their century-old 'West Country Litany' – a prayer for protection!

From Ghoulies and Ghosties
And long leggety beasties
And things that go Bump in the Night
Good Lord, deliver us.

The credulous claim that this little prayer is a powerful talisman against untoward influences.

The caves, ravines, rock and heather-clad Mendips offer a bountiful myths and extraordinary challenges for those daring explorers of strange situations and places. From the M5 motorway, as one wends past Junction 21, the Mendips become a familiar site, stretching for thirty miles from Frome to Weston-super-Mare, where the Phrygian cap of Crook's Peak makes a characteristic marker point. Geographically, they have been described as a small mountain range. In Mendips, many caves with prehistoric human and animal remains have been discovered; the bones of reindeer, mammoth and woolly rhinoceros included. Saxon and Norman fought ferocious battles, and before them the Romans mined for lead. History has bequeathed a trail of ghosts, more so at Priddy where the shadowy figures of past mine workers and soldiers still travel the ancient byways.

A villager retold the famous legend of the boy Jesus coming to this place, 'There's ancient spirits, some robed in eastern garb, walk these places, coming back to remember, and others just was once a part of it all', he said. Among Mendip hill folk, this arcane lore is just as alive now as yesteryear. In 1947, Cyril C. Dobson remarked:

… and Rev. H.A. Lewis writes: 'Anyone who really seeks can find abundant evidence that it was a household tradition at Priddy in the last generation that Christ came there, while it is certain that there is an age-old proverb in parts of the Mendip, "As sure as our Lord was at Priddy". It is more than probable that Blake was referring to this in his poem:

"And did those feet in ancient time,
Walk upon England's mountains green?"'

Ray Gibbs, describing one of the islands of Somerset's 'valley of the kings' states:

The Godney Chapel had a particularly quaint tale. Its ancient chapel was said to have been so sacred and holy that 'even the birds of the air did not foul it, nor the island upon which it stood, and so it was in ancient times called *Insula Dei* or God's Island … which almost without saying, has an incredible atmosphere, and accounts of a long boat carrying a sacred corpse to be interred there … but the hidden tradition that this was Joseph of Aramathea has been discounted by one family's oral knowledge.

Some aspects of this legend are said to be even more religiously explosive than the *Da Vinci Code*.

Discarnate entities supposedly roam and make themselves felt by either fleeting shapes or unpleasant sounds at Burrington Cavern. A skull and several skeletons have been discovered.

That regal sentinel, the huge Lion Rock rises above the entrance of Cheddar Gorge ravine. Cheddar Caves are among Somerset's most tourist thronged centres. Then again, there are those who say that these fabulous caverns, festooned with mystically-tinted stalactites, have their unique phantoms of great antiquity. Sceptics might prefer to partake of the town's virtually unrivalled cheddar cheese; and please mind the gaunt silhouette of the lady 'who disappears' on a seat near the stream.

The hamlet of Charterhouse asserts quite a Roman heritage, though prehistory looms never far with hills dotted with ancient and allegedly very haunted tumuli. Once again, the wraiths of Roman soldiers have been mentioned by late walkers, local ramblers and visitors. Archaeological evidence has revealed its importance as a centre for silver and lead mining by the Iberians and the Belgae. Earthworks confirm their final resting places; now they are centuries defunct except for the ghosts.

'I was working near a wild spot close to the Mendip Hills', recalled a Clevedon man, to the ghost researcher Petronella O'Donnell. It was during the late 1900s, and one morning he thought to go out of his way and take a road over the Mendips to his work:

This would mean a walk of several miles but I was young and I felt I wanted some adventure. I had to rise more than an hour earlier that morning to do the walk in time and I took a stout stick with me. It was a beautiful walk, just a narrow path that lost itself every now and again, but a longer walk than I had imagined. I came all of a sudden to an open space and beyond that wild bushes, trees and grasses, and two great iron gates looking as if they led to some big mansion beyond. I was so surprised I stood still, and as I stood still a black rabbit ran out of the big gates. Such a big black rabbit it were and the thought came into my mind, evil like, what a supper it would make for me. I lifted my stick to strike it when I heard the sound of horse's hoofs coming at a mighty big pace I was surprised I can tell you to hear that at such an hour and in such a place. I turned round to see what it was and like a flash a hearse with a pair of black horses, more like devils they were, their ears all peaked up, their eyes like fire, tore past me. The driver was the most awful person I ever did put my eyes on, like the Devil himself. It was all gone by in a flash and I was all of a shake.

When he nervously confided to a retired countryman, he was taken aback by the unexpected reply:

You ain't the only one who has seen the hearse and the rabbit. Why scores of us have seen it, when we've been silly like to go over that there hill path in the early morning … all the folks in this part know of the hearse and rabbit I can tell 'ee.

Love Invisible

'Take it or leave it, but I know what I felt and I know what I saw', said the retired teacher, a silver-haired and sun-tanned countryman, adding:

She taught at my school. Primrose pretty, golden hair and blue-grey eyes. A little woman, slim and always on the move. Soft, musical voice. Very Somerset, though. Taught mainly English, with geography and history thrown in. Hobbies? She flew a kite up on Brent Knoll. Now, there's a book, alone. 'Come on, you've been up there many a walk with your old dog. Surely you have sensed the knoll's power?'

Brent Knoll – scene of an ethereal love story.

Beyond this huge earth rise, the moors and water levels were once sea sunken. This green and undulating bowl has become a melting pot of folk beliefs and quaint customs. Over 457ft high, the views are wonderful. Embedded in its girth can still be seen the marks and outlines of Roman fortifications. It was used as a beacon – Brent means 'burnt'. One story relates how King Alfred battled the Danes on its vast flanks.

It is, of course, a place of exceptional atmosphere, but that summer day's interest circled the school teacher, and we shall call her 'Vera'. Shortly before her death, she confided in her colleague the uncanny reason for remaining unmarried.

Vera was fascinated with this conical beacon, said to have been a giant clod, sent flying from Cheddar as the Devil (another name for the Norse deity Odin, Saxon: Woden) dug out the famous gorge. Vera could not avoid the supernatural beliefs that were also awash around this major landmark between the Mendips and the Poldens, overseeing the marshes of the river Brue and encompassing the distant Glastonbury Tor. 'It is easy to scoff at legends and ghost stories'. Vera is alleged to have said:

> … places like this are full of ghosts, coming, going and staying, mingling with everyone. They murmur a reminder of their memories. They are from all parts of history. This is where I fell in love with Leonard … well, that is how he whispered his name.

The old teacher related how that day Vera was flying her kite from atop Brent Knoll when she was astonished to see another, cross-shaped kite join her own squared canvas. It drifted away, but as it did, she was overwhelmed by a physical presence by her side and heard a barely audible voice call, 'Leonard. It's me, Len'. Vera called him her 'ghost lover' and would walk and sit on top of the hill for many hours, to all accounts talking to someone else. The teacher said:

> All said, Vera passed away shortly after her retirement but not before she told me her story. By the way, she also said that the Knoll was often quite busy with a variety of ghosts, and that some resembled young children. A couple of months ago, I was walking my dog. Lovely, bright day and I had, so to speak, the hill to myself. Or, so thought, when to my surprise, I found myself watching a large, box-like kite swinging high in the sky. Its line was dangling loose, and I can promise you, there was no human hand guiding it. As I was saying early on, take it or leave it … but there's others will tell you some odd tales about Brent Knoll.

Haunted Stogursey

There's a saying, 'out of the world and into Stogursey', which aside from its absorbing paranormal tales, has another local claim to fame – it was once represented by two members of Parliament.

Stoke Courcy dates to the Norman period under the auspices of Norman noble, William de Falaise. The faery-tale castle stands robustly amid a moat. Its roundhouse is supposedly haunted by several 'half-formed' figures, including a monk. It is also recorded that a well-dressed horseman is the ghost of King John who used to hunt there. Nearby Cole Pool is said to be bottomless. Memories of giants and pixies throng local legends and are said to occupy centuries -old earthen mounds in the outer vicinity.

The magnificent Priory church of St Andrew is associated with numerous strange events, particularly The Dead House, the remains of which stand in the south-west corner of the church

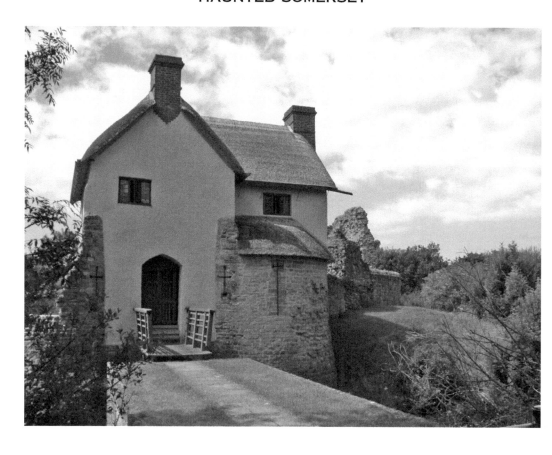

Above and left: *Stogursey Castle – haunt of mysterious figures.*

yard. It was built in 1867 'to distribute parish relief, store coal and to receive strange dead', which included 'unknown bodies washed ashore until an inquest had been held', says a local brochure. Apparently, the place is earmarked by ghost hunters as a place of unearthly activities.

During the 1920s and 30s, an author with psychic interests, Petronella O'Donnell, wrote many articles about Somerset's folk beliefs. Here, she discusses Stogursey, '… we went on to the wild parts of Somerset. I remarked that I should think some parts of the county were haunted and in other parts I knew that fairies had been seen. There is a Pixie Field at Stogursey for example'.

Ghosts of Crime

In 1775, the city of Bath was still proclaiming its Georgian architectural splendour in tandem with a glamorous phase of high-society partying, celebrity visits from poets, writers and actors. At the same time, barely a two-hour horse ride away, a very nasty event was happening in a pastoral place.

If it is true that brutal murders leave creepy memories and violent 'psychic imprints', then it is understandable why three female ghosts have been witnessed wandering near the spot of what little remains of their 1700s cottage in the tiny hamlet of Woodford within Monksilver's picturesque combe. In the Monksilver churchyard, a tombstone relates their unsolved murders:

> In Memory of Mrs. Elizabeth Conibeer aged Eighty Eight years. And her Two daughters Anne aged Forty five and Sarah forty three who was all inhumanly Murdered in the Day of the 5th June 1775 in their House in Woodford in this Parish.

> Inhuman wretch, whoer thou art,
> That dids't commit this Heinous crime,
> Repent before thou dost depart,
> To meet thine awful Judge Divine.

Elizabeth Conibeer and her two daughters, Ann and Sarah, were local dressmakers and immensely popular souls. It is no wonder this place is so haunted, because in its time, it was a terrible murder.

It is also no surprise that this grisly event has to this day, left a depressing and menacing atmosphere around where the cottage once stood. In recent years, a female figure has been seen walking down the lane towards the Conibeer home. No one else has been able to confirm a once 'confidential account', of a young man's figure, seen hastening from the place, only to fade in the air. Who was he? Was he the youth who discovered the bodies? Was he their killer?

Having lunched in that overcast summer's day, the three ladies talked as they awaited the arrival of the local baker's boy, with money on the table ready to pay the bill; money that was later discovered not to have been stolen. On arriving at the old house, the boy beheld a scene of carnage. Blood was everywhere, and the bodies of the three Conibeers lay with terrible injuries. Writing in the *West Somerset Year Book*, 1938, Clement E. Kille graphically describes what happened:

> Picture a sunny morning (in June 1775), a baker's lad whistling merrily as with laden basket on his arm, he kicked open the garden gate and approached the cottage door where he was accustomed to leave the daily ration. He knocked, but no one replied: this was unusual, and, the door being

ajar, he pushed it gently, when a horrible sight made his eyes bulge! Everything seemed to be spattered with blood, and the three women whom he knew so well, lay sprawled about the floor of their living-room with ugly bleeding gashes on their bodies. He gaped, then ran as if possessed by the Devil to the nearest neighbours and spread the ghastly news. A large pair of tailor's shears, lying on the table, smothered in blood, proclaimed itself as the weapon with which the crime was committed. The bodies were warm; it was evident that the murderer could not possibly have got far away, but no sign of him was found. Some there were who would have accused the baker, but no proof could be laid against him; his straight-forward manner and the fact that he had so promptly reported the crime were in his favour. It was afterwards surmised that he himself had a narrow escape for it was believed that when he called, the murderer was hiding in the house.

Unfortunately for the rustic spirits of the Conibeers, their killer was never discovered. Doubtless many a contemporary crime researcher could find plentiful scope in attempting to solve this tragic jigsaw puzzle. Thus said, there exists a less debated reason for the Conibeer crime – witchcraft. Folklorist Ruth Tongue wrote:

> … found brutally cut about by a pair of tailor's shears, may have been a ritual bloodletting to break a spell, or may have started with that intention. At least I have heard it hinted in districts fifteen miles apart … that these women had brought their killing upon themselves. The murderer was never found, but the local people knew who it was.

Unusual 'faces' of an elderly woman were fashioned by light and shade when photographs of the grave stone were taken for this book. Other female faces have been pointed out. Are they tricks of shadow and lichen? Perhaps they are what some paranormal devotees would call 'photo aports'?

The Conibeer grave. Possibly a trick of the light, but image of an elderly lady can be made out, among other female silhouettes.

Cooked Curate

The persistence of a ghostly 'man of the cloth' comes as no surprise. It is one of Somerset's most macabre murders on record. Although this grisly event happened in 1624, the gentleman's 'outline' has been seen in recent years near Cleeve church and also Cleeve Abbey.

'Many people have told me that when they go for a walk from Old Cleeve to Blue Anchor they often hear other footsteps on the road and yet when they stop to ascertain who is following them, they see and hear nothing', wrote author Alan Holt about the unseen rustles and noises often heard by hill walkers on this lonely stretch. It is believed to be the ghost of one or more of the four murderers who slew the Revd Mr Trat, curate to the rector of Old Cleeve, the Revd Edward Brickenden.

In truth, it is bloodcurdling. It would never have been discovered but for a twist of fate and the eye of a Norfolk researcher, who finding the evidence in a 1744 chapbook stowed in an East Herling church chest, sent a copy to an 'interested party' in Somerset – or so one is led to assume. Later scrutiny of local archives uncovered the nitty gritties of the curate's ghastly demise. Some of the chapbook's age-withered pages were titled *The Crying Murder*, containing the cruel and most horrible butchery of Mr Trat, curate of Old Cleeve, who was first murdered as he travelled upon the highway, then was brought home to his house, quartered and disembowelled; his quarters and bowels being afterwards boiled and 'salted up, in a most strange and fearful manner' – echoing the biblical, 'Eat of my blood, eat of my flesh'. Trat's flesh, cured by salting, drained of blood then separated into a container to be boiled by Alice Walker conjures up the sheer hatred and sacrifice involved. Was this a communal feast?

The chapbook read, 'For this fact the Judgement of my Lord Chief Baron Tanfield – young Peter Smethwicke, Andrew Baker, Cyril Austen and Alice Walker were executed at this last Summer Assizes, the 24 July, at Stone Gallows, near Taunton in Somersetshire 1624'. Why? A pagan ritual sacrifice? After all, the Old Religion was powerfully operative in remote rural districts, particularly during the 1600-1700s.

Local parish and judicial records unveil a profound bitterness between Trat and many of his parishioners, mostly for being a severe stickler to the Ten Commandments, which he felt should be obeyed to the letter. Court records show that Trat's outspoken sermons created anger and feelings of revenge; perhaps he was hinting that he knew too much about the moral or other behaviour of certain church members. Interestingly, rigid Christian dogma was reaching another one of its hysterical anti-witchcraft peaks, and adherents of the old beliefs could still vent (and did) their wrath on overtly zealous priests.

Tantalisingly coincidental, Trat's dismemberment occurred on or around fourth of July's St John's Eve, the old Summer Witch Feast. He had also been accused of being the cause of his wife's death, who drowned at Blue Anchor after being cut off by the rising tide. When next the congregation heard that he would be taking over as rector, panic set loose, and four parishioners, including the grandson of the incumbent rector, plotted to remove him – head, torso, arms, legs and internal organs – so that no evidence survived his demise.

Within two weeks, his 'absence' led law officers of the time to discover Peter Smethwicke's coat in Trat's house. They also found a pot of blood and charred bones. Giving chase to another suspect, Cyril Austin, the constables found him with a portion of blood-stained cloth in his pocket, metaphorically, a 'trophy'. All four accused were unrepentant. Taunton's stone gallows finally felt their guilt. But, the ghosts haven't stopped roaming that remote road. It has even been claimed that certain members of the deeply angered community supped on the curate's well-cooked remains.

The area surrounding Walford's haunted gibbet.

The White Foxes

White foxes are still seen on the Quantocks. They are believed to be the guardian spirits of the dead. This brings us to a sensational murder and its extraordinary aftermath, which still grips the imagination of locals and tourists.

The twenty-four-year-old corpse of John Walford, a charcoal burner, described as a kindly, honest man from the village of Over Stowey, was left to decompose on the oaken gibbet for a year, which ironically stood facing the cottage of Walford's stepmother. This shows how determined the authorities were to set an example. His remains were buried 10ft below what became known as Walford's Gibbet.

After his three-hour trial at Bridgwater Assize on 18 August 1789 by Lord Kenyon, he was found guilty of murdering a 'simple country girl', Jane Thorney, whom he had married after she had enticed him to make love, subsequently falling pregnant. They married, but within five weeks he had struck her with a hedge post, then cut her throat after quarrelling as they strolled across romantic wayside paths to the Castle of Comfort Inn. There are numerous theories as to why they quarrelled, but it was doubtless a loveless short marriage because it was widely known that John Walford had been desperate to marry the love of his heart, Ann Rice, a miller's daughter. Elsewhere, it was recalled that Walford's possessive stepmother opposed the marriage, and it was called off.

The Castle of Comfort Inn.

An extract from the *Weekly Entertainer*, Sherborne, Dorset, 7 September 1789 states:

His trial came on before Lord Kenyon at Bridgwater, on Tuesday the 18th of August, and lasted about three hours, during which time upwards of ten Witnesses were called, whose evidence fully satisfied his Lordship and the Jury that he was the perpetrator of the horrid deed … Tears trickled down the venerable cheeks of the Judge while he endeavoured to awaken him to a sense of his duty; the whole court seemed more affected than the Prisoner himself, for sullen he first appeared and so remained to the last. The grand jury petitioned for him to be hung in chains near the spot where the murder happened, which request was granted. After condemnation he confessed that he did the murder, and that he intended to have thrown her Body into the copper mine, but he could not move it from the ground. On Thursday the 20th of August, he was drawn from Bridgwater to a place called Dodington Common (being part of Quantock Hill); he was taken to the very spot where his wife was found dead, from whence he was drawn about a quarter of a mile up the hill, and was there executed on a temporary gallows, amidst perhaps the greatest number of spectators that ever were assembled on the like occasion in the neighbourhood, supposed to be no less than 3000!

Before his execution at Bincombe, overlooking Dodington village, he was briefly reunited with Ann Rice, who was allowed several minutes with him before he was hoisted to death.

Over the years, many local folk say that have met the form of a young man, in a charcoal burner's attire. Others mention an inexplicable feeling of sadness where once the gibbet stood. Walking and talking is the only way to discover local knowledge. On a warm, sunny Easter Sunday afternoon, directions for Walford's Gibbet confirmed its position. His former dwelling is still in line with where he hung all those long years ago, though now converted into an outbuilding.

Thomas Poole wrote an eye-witness account of the Walford tragedy. If ever there was a local celebrity, it was Thomas Poole of Nether Stowey, who has been described as very well educated and a fount of charitable kindness. Born at Nether Stowey in 1765, Poole occupied a huge Georgian-style house in Castle Street where he entertained many leading poets, essayists and scholars of the day, including Wordsworth and Coleridge. At one point, Poole adds a movingly mysterious twist to Walford's saga:

> Two white foxes were said to have guarded the body when it was in the cage, the villagers would not go near the spot after dark for years. A woman in black was said to walk the road at Shervage Woods, and many people claimed to have seen her including Mr A. Luttrell, who saw her one night while walking to East Quantoxhead, she walked a little way along the road, and then disappeared into the woods, but at that time Mr. Luttrell thought it was a real woman, and took little notice until friends pointed out to him that he must have seen 'Jenny' for this was the woman in black.

Poetic Ghosts

The renowned poet, Alfred Lord Tennyson, whose links with Clevedon are well documented, wrote a haunting poem called *The Grandmother*. Widely acclaimed Minehead poet, Rosemary Burnett, contributes Mr Fern:

> With a child's curiosity,
> I often pondered
> the long-term spinsterhood
> of my favourite great-aunt.
> She never assuaged that enquiry
> well, not as much as I'd have liked.
> With a smile bordering on smugness,
> I had to rest content
> with the archly mysterious:
> 'Not for want of being asked!'
>
>
> Persistent wheedling on my part
> proved of no avail until
> one day of rare confidence
> Great-Aunt let slip her suitor,
> one Mr Fern, who lived upstairs.

Frequent though my visits were,
never once, to my intense chagrin,
did I glimpse Mr. Fern,
only heard a firm football,
unwavering on each creaking rise.

Crimson and viridian add drama now
to the drab London brick, overshadowed
by Upton Park football ground.
The house, they tell me, is owned
by an Asian lady of uncertain years.
Does she, I wonder, hear the spectral tread
of lovelorn Mr Fern upon the stairs?

Gallows Oak

Chard's Gallows Oak was cut down in the 1800s, but has not lost its nerve-jangling status. Old Chard folk still recall the talk of figures hanging from its boughs. Twelve Chard men who fought in the Monmouth rebellion were hanged from its spreading branches, including the Duke of Monmouth's own body servant, and it is said, James Durnett, the son-in-law of John Bunyan as well.

One of the earliest plate photographs of Chard's Gallows Oak, published locally in 1839, was captured by the inventor of the first aeroplane, John Stringfellow. Several of its largest branches reached over 40ft, almost horizontally from the fork, and on these muscled limbs the Monmouth rebels were hung.

The Uninvited

'Intensely eerie' would describe Francis Harriet Wood's personal summary of her experiences in the late 1800s, after moving into Abbey Grange called Street House, near Glastonbury.

Previous owners had reported that it was an exceptionally troubled home, harassed by more than one nightmarish guest. Harriet wrote, 'My father had, however, made up his mind there was no truth in the tales told ... No one spoke to us of ghosts, the servants having been warned it would mean instant dismissal ...' Nevertheless, the moment Harriet saw the outstretched hand of a robed figure, heard the arrival of an invisible carriage stop in the drive, a violent knocking at the back door, as well as the numinous shape of a white dog, she became convinced that bizarre influences were afoot.

Other family members said they had seen a nun 'quite visible'. Harriet added that the cook, '... many years after told us she used to often see a little old man in a leathern jerkin, with knee breeches, in the old scullery'. In spite of this formidable accumulation of phantasms and other disturbances, Harriet said that they, 'lived at Street House for a quarter of a century in great happiness.'

Spooky Wookey

'Father, such a funny old man comes to see me every night; he has a coat with gold buttons like yours, and a tail down from his head', said the eldest son to his father, a Naval Admiral. The family was residing at Wookey House during the 1800s. Also, the boy's father said he too had seen this same apparition as a child. Long after the family had left the area, a relative met a servant at Wookey House, telling how a guest had seen the same ghost tumbling down the garden well. Would-be rescuers found nothing but a pile of stones at the well's bottom. Clergy from Wells Cathedral held a special service and the restless spirit was laid to rest.

'Phantasy and the Supernatural in Folk Lore' was the lecture by Miss M.B. Jennings to the Society of Somerset Folk's Arts Circle in 1923. One of her topics included another side to the famed Cheddar and Wookey Hole, or Cavern.

Cheddar's southern slope of the Mendip Hills features the prehistoric Gough's and Cox's caves – named after the local men who discovered them. Millions of tourists visit Wookey Caves to sightsee its dramatic antiquity. New owner, Gerry Cottle, of circus-name fame, hopes to eventually have the bones of the legendary Witch of Wookey, currently housed in the Wells Museum, returned to be displayed.

As usually expected, plenty of creepy gossip surrounds this ancient place, said to be haunted by England's oldest ghost, the Witch, mentioned in Percy's *Reliques*:

Deep in a dreamy dismal cell,
Which seemed, and was ycleped, hell,
This blear-eyed hag did hide.

An oddly jutting stone formation is pointed out to resemble the witch. Other shapes are said to be her demons. Feared throughout Somerset as a once voluptuous woman who made a pact with the Devil, she terrorised the county. Eventually, a young monk challenged her and as she rushed screeching towards him, he gave her a thorough soaking with holy water. Through the sizzling and hissing sound of the water's spiritual power, the witch, along with her demonic creatures, froze into stone. That is just one version of what happened.

Eerie Exmoor

Whether in sunlight or moonlight, Exmoor exudes verses of colour, an unforgettable splendour of combe, heath and woodlands that sweep down to meet the Atlantic echoes that touch rocky bays, sandy shores and pebbled beaches. It has, for bygones, inspired the pens of poets and palettes of artists. Nonetheless, there exists another side to this exotic region of undulating rapture – the realm of witches, goblins and ghosts

Likewise, the moor's towns and villages, themselves engraved upon ancestral roots, are brimming with tantalising signs and omens. 'People believed that stags and hares were often possessed with evil spirits …' noted Walter W. Joyce in *Moorside Talks and Tales*. In my dozens of interviews and 'listenings' throughout the shire, it is clear that the majority of superstitious beliefs and practices were, for whatever reasons, concocted to ward away ghosts and malevolent pixies – and whatever else could 'go bump in the night'. A more modern bedtime petition for protection goes something like this: 'Lord keep us safe this night, secure from all our fears, and may angels guard us while we sleep 'til morning light appears'. Grim goings-on have kept Exmoor under the ghostly spotlight, so here we may savour a handful of the moor's perplexing spooks. Who would ever have guessed that a walk across Exmoor is to tempt troublesome or perhaps even impish spirits?

Then there is the ghost of a Carter, making abrupt appearances on misty nights at the ancient Caractacus standing stone. Word of mouth recalls that the Carter tried to dig beneath the stone and unearth its legendary buried treasure. Unfortunately, the stone fell on him and he died almost instantly. The name Caractacus is of Romano-Celtic origin, though some archaeologists believe it pre-dates Roman activity. Its carved motif inscribes *Caracti (N) Epus*. Whether this refers to the Welsh King St Caractacus, stands an open question. Other beliefs say that the spot is visited by a phantom wagon and horses.

Hawkridge boasts a long history of people, gifted with healing powers and 'second-sight'. No one can identify the alleged grave of a local man, who made nightly returns to his former home. Village memory records that the parson ended up leading the ghost to some nearby hilly and tree-covered ground, where they shook hands, and the already departed soul melted in a flash of light, never to return.

The Tarr Thing

The crystal music of the river Barle flows agelessly below the Tarr, or Tor Steps. Nevertheless its enthralling beauty reflects an uneasy enchantment. Legend says that 'the Devil himself' created them. Whatever one believes, there are lots of puzzles associated with this 2,000-yr old bridge.

Former British Airways administrative staff member, the late Paul Simmons, in tandem with his partner, Helen, were spending a week on Exmoor, 'simply for a well-earned rest'. 'We were excited to be visiting the Tarr Steps'. From the road, Helen exclaimed 'What the hell is that?!'

It was bright sunlight and around 4pm, because I remember that we were tight on time. It was the shape of a man, naked and covered in hair, but half of his body was missing! Try telling people that! To cut the story short, I tried to take a photo, but it had disappeared. Obviously, and ever since, we have tried to find out more, but were only told and read that the steps were prehistoric, so maybe the figure is a clue to that part of history.'

All the journalist Lornie Leete-Hodge could ascertain was that 'the actual date of its construction has not been determined. But it is an ancient packhorse bridge, 180-ft long with seventeen spans. Legend claims the Devil built it and one tale says that a cat, running across it, disappeared in a puff of sulphur!'

'Room for the Night, Sir?'

Another turn up for the books must be the rarely mentioned, but decidedly spooked, seventeenth-century watering hole at historic Kilve. The Hood has a well-starred name for fine cuisine against a setting of original oak beams and open fireplaces. Owned and managed by Barry and Vanessa Eason and family, it once boasted its own off-road chapel, which was demolished during the 1950s.

Although Barry has not seen their secret resident, he was happy to confirm that some folk

The Hood Arms – Room 6 is said to have a ghostly occupant.

claim to have seen the shadowy figure of a female in 'Room 6', he said with a smile.

Few innkeepers lack a spooky yarn, and Somerset pubs abound with stories of sightings and sounds from the 'otherworld'. The Holman Clavel Inn, near Taunton, is supposedly the focus for a skittle-playing spook. Also, strange music, some say a violin, has been heard in certain bedrooms at Taunton's Castle Hotel. A cavalier has been said to manifest at King Charles Parlour, Wells Street. So, pubs, inns and hotels provide huge opportunities for hungry ghost hunters. However, be wary of where you rest your head at night because not all of Somerset's invisible visitors are particularly nice.

There are also certain innkeepers who fight shy of publicity. 'We don't want to put off potential custom, do we now?' said the swarthy owner of a Mid-Somerset Inn, adding:

… but trusting you in confidence, I'll tell you about one of our double-guest, en-suite rooms, which has an extremely nasty tale to it … and I'm still thinking about changing it back to storage area, so that no one else has to suffer. How we've kept it out of the press, beats me.

Here is the story, almost word for word:

We moved here some years now. As you can see, it's fairly historic. Spent a lot on refurbishment, the dining space, the gardens, the kitchen and whatever. And all was well, business soon speeded

Taunton Castle – ghostly music.

up, and by our second summer, we were taking more guests. The previous landlord told us to leave the big storage room alone, being useful for just that, storage. Anyway, we used an outhouse for storage and converted the space into a double suite.

One autumn morning, a couple booked out, without warning. While her partner was up and down loading their car, I asked the lady if anything was wrong. 'Wrong!' she gasped. 'We've had a really nasty experience in that room. Tell me, do you believe in ghosts?' I could hardly believe my ears. 'Yes and no, why?' She lowered her voice.

'Last night we were both woken by a loudish thump. Jim put on the table light. Regardless of the light, this awful "thing" just wouldn't go away. It was a withered, very thin, stooped old man, and he was sort of drifting through the air towards us with his hands outstretched as if to strangle us. His face was covered in hair. We flung ourselves out of bed, and Jim rushed at him, but through him. It was 4.20 in the morning. Anyway, we did not sleep and have decided that we can't possibly stay. I am so sorry, but I think you need to look into the history of this place.

'And, did you?'

'To be honest, I thought they were trying it on, wanted a free stay. Since then, two more couples told me the same. So, we're going to re-convert back to storage. I haven't seen nor heard anything myself. I love this place and no ghost is going to get us to move. We did ask a local if he'd ever heard that the inn was haunted. He said he hadn't.'

The Choughs at Chard.

Four centuries old, The Choughs at Chard has more than earned its name as a tavern for psychic phenomena and other peculiar episodes. Chard, along with its numerous inns and boarding houses, is among the oldest towns in Somerset, which is said to have been named after the West Saxon leader, Cerdic. Even with modernity's changes, Chard can boast some fine examples of sixteenth-century architecture. The Choughs, a gabled building, is a hotel of charm and comfort. However, there is what some might call 'a darker or supernatural side' to the place, which in turn has unearthed some notable mysteries.

Over the centuries, customers and guests have described the image of an unpleasant looking old man frequenting the fireplace. Voices and whisperings have been heard in a central upstairs room, as one particular guest told the owners, but they denied any knowledge of what it might be or mean. On returning some years later, the woman related the event to the new landlord, who confirmed that she was not the only guest to have experienced ghosts doing whatever they are destined to do in the night – in fact, even in the day.

The landlord also said that during renovations, what appeared to be a thick wall running along the 'disturbed room' concealed a smaller room, believed to have been a ladies' retiring chamber. Other structural work has brought to light an age-weathered tombstone, with the barely detectable carved word 'Winifred' sunk upside down into the fireplace. Guesswork is still rife as to its origin. Also, there are reports of glasses being swiftly moved off the counter and shadowy figures being seen.

St Audries – A coffin has been sighted on this stretch of road.

Mind the Road

Certain roads, paths and tracks can be forbidding, even treacherous in more ways than one. The county is a veritable ghost hunter's delight, and anybody planning to delve into 'the unusual', should not bypass any part of Somerset and its vast vistas of exquisite landscapes and lost hamlets, where even today modernity has not too severely trespassed. But beware if you put out at night because you could come across some strange encounters on the region's unlit, lonely tracks and roads. Oral and written tales abound, and in particular the road to Bridgwater from Watchet is notable for the manifestation of a coffin in the middle of the highway between St Audries and Kilve. And, if you're lucky, or unlucky enough to see this chilly sight, you might even run into the Devil in full gallop, leading a pack of baying hounds! The A39 is rated as a highly haunted stretch of road.

Julian Bruford's compilation *A History of Part of West Somerset*, reviewing the Quantocks and its surroundings, and originally in written notes, mentions some of the local beliefs and superstitions:

> The Devil is said to ride over Putsham Hill every night at midnight, perhaps on his way to his hunting ground at Cannington Park, where he joins his headless companions mounted on

phantom horses and followed by a ghostly pack of hounds. Legend says that he used to stop at the Devil's Forge at Keenthorn to have a shoe fitted, but why was this necessary is beyond me for his horse always gallops a few feet from the ground, and when hunting the whole hunt flies in mid air. It is said that the monks at Cannington gave colour to this tale, no doubt that they half believed it for they erected a Rood across the lane leading to the park ... thieves and poachers gave it a wide berth and would not go near the park at night! In the country folk always saw the Devil as a countryman who was either riding a horse or driving a coach ... In medieval times the Devil played a great part in church life, and slowly took the form of a man with forked tail, horns growing from the head and cloven hooves.

In 1952, a bus driver said that the ghost horses on Porlock Hill 'are grey.' Locals say that a coach overturned when the horses bolted, ran away and were killed. There are also descriptions from car drivers of a coach and horses following their vehicles along the Minehead road, near the turn to Dunster. Dressed in modern casual clothes, a number of motorists have insisted that they have seen a young man 'thumbing a lift' next to the lane that leads to Nunney Castle. On stopping to offer him a lift, he disappears.

Girl with a Comb

Unwelcome storms made many rural roads impassable, and whether travelling by stagecoach or horseback, came the perils of 'the gentlemen of the road' – highwaymen. Many countryfolk could not afford horse or coach and walked for miles to reach their destination. Unless unavoidable, few folk set out in a Somerset sunset or 'dimmet', for fear of meeting another threat ... spooks.

Local preachers were great walkers, covering many miles as they visited town and village, a trend especially encouraged by John Wesley, who arrived in Somerset on 31 March 1739 to 'spread the Gospel'. During the winter of 1847–48, a local Wesleyan preacher, Thomas Taylor March, walking the highway between West Chinnock and Crewkerne, came across a young woman sitting in the middle of the road. March wrote in the 1870 Christmas edition of *Pulman's Weekly News* that the woman:

> ... had on a loose white dress. She was engaged in combing her hair on the right side of her head and her face was turned towards the left. On getting up to her, I paused and remarked that she had chosen a cold berth. Receiving no response, I bade her 'good night' and passed on. I looked back, after going some little way, and saw her in the same position, still combing her hair. My first impression was that she was one of a party of young persons, and that it was a very silly lark. But seeing no one else on my road to Crewkerne, I concluded that she must be a poor maniac, and charged myself with inhumanity for not rendering assistance.
>
> I related the whole circumstances to my wife on my return home, and she has still a vivid recollection of it. I also spoke of it to many persons in the neighbourhood, who supposed that it must have been a practical joke.

Strangely, the editor of *The Western Gazette*, Mr G. F. Munford, had already interviewed a local resident some nineteen years earlier about the same apparition. He recounted an almost identical experience:

An electrical sensation which I shall never forget! Although it would be impossible to describe – stole over me. The blood tingled in my veins, and I could feel that my hat was being lifted off my head by the unwilling agency of my own hair. Afraid to face the figure any longer, I tore myself away at the top of my speed, which I did not relax until fairly out of breath … whilst I ploughed through the slush I thought I heard a woman's wailing voice borne along by the boisterous wind – 'Oh why does he not come? Why does he not come?'

It later emerged that Ellen, the only daughter of a local farmer, had arranged to marry at Christmas 1851. A month before, young Harry Gill, Ellen's fiancé, riding home from Sandy Road was thrown from his horse and killed. The shock of the news drove her insane and several weeks after the tragedy Ellen's drowned body was found floating in a pool of water on a piece of wasteland. Clothed in her night dress, one of her hands gripped a hair comb.

The Dark Riders

If you don't believe that ghostly highwaymen continue to roam our rustic byways, then be warned. Another tale concerns a local man journeying to Crewkerne from Chard. In worsening snow and in cold and howling wind, he arrived outside a cottage, where a nervous couple directed him on to Purtington. Near a crossroads at Blackmoor Copse, he heard a spine-tingling scream as a ghostly, riderless horse, followed by another, ridden by a cloaked figure carrying a pistol; and then by a third in fast pursuit, raced through the darkness.

Stretch of the Crewkerne-Chard road where a ghostly pursuit has been seen.

The ghost of a phantom hitchhiker has been reported along this span of the A38 Taunton-Minehead road.

He told his tale of the fearsome scene to the folk of Coombe Farm Valley. No one disagreed about the details, and the locals then told of what they knew. One figure was of a notorious smuggler who had slain two coastguardsmen, who were the other ghosts in hot chase. Apparently, this haunting occurs regularly … especially during a wintry moonlit night.

Devil's Drive

So, it does pay to mind certain roads in Somerset; that is, if you are forearmed with what might lay ahead! This little known memento is well worth quoting, witnessed in 1893 by a certain Mr G.F.R.

Adjoining the town and in the parish of Yeovil there is a well-know plantation called Newton Copse, the greater part of which forms a steep decline from the top of a high hill called Summer House Hill to the highway below called Newton Road, leading from the town of Yeovil to the villages of Stolford, Barwick and others. A footpath parallel to Newton Road also runs through the middle of the copse. The plantation is thickly planted with trees, except in one part of it where there is apparently a natural avenue formed, leading from the top of the hill to the road beneath and crossing the footpath at right angles. Mr G.F.R. noted:

This avenue, at the time I knew it, was quite wide enough to allow a carriage and four being driven thro' it, but it was then over grown with grass, and did not appear to have been ever used as a road or way. Moreover it was so steep that it was evident that any ordinary mortal who attempted to drive down over it would come to grief. Nevertheless it was called the 'Devil's Drive' and in the days of my early youth I have often listened in awe to the weird tales that were told me concerning it.

It was said that trees would not ever grow on the land which formed the site of this avenue, that the Devil and some of his kindred spirits were often to be seen at certain hours of the night, and more especially at that witching time 'when churchyards yawn.' … that once on a time one of the townsmen, having occasion to go through the copse in the middle of the night, had suddenly met with his Satanic majesty taking his usual drive. Not only was the townsman very much alarmed at such an unusual spectacle, but it seems the spirits did not at all like the interruption … I have now long since left the neighbourhood, but the story still remains deeply impressed on my memory.

Could some sightings of an unearthly hitchhiker be nothing more than a straggle of hedge, which to many motorists seem to mimic a human form stepping towards the road or 'hitching a lift', particularly at dusk or in misty weather? This is not to decry the now legendary reports of the A38 phantom hitchhiker, a firmly believed-in phantom, whose roadside appearances near Taunton, have won considerable space in the local press since the 1950s. Seen by many motorists, one lorry driver told a reporter that he had seen the man in 1958, carrying a torch. The phantom wears a grey overcoat. Considering the very large number of fatal accidents along the A38, it is surprising that there are not many more 'returning souls'.

Coffin Lid

There are recollections of a man carrying a coffin lid on a path below Clevedon's Dial Hill. For many years, up to the present, Dial Hill has an eerie name for unexpected happenings. One of the most stirring, is the chilling sight of a headless horseman who canters his black steed along a nearby lane.

Beasties

Hearsay of vapourish animals or others appearing in clear form come from village, town and countryside. Black dogs, galloping horses, birds and other beasties also crop up throughout the UK. Budleigh Hill, Winsford Hill, Dulverton, Weacombe, Exmoor, the coast road from St Audries to Perry Farm and the Selworthy-Tivington crossroads are worth noting for catching sight of these legendary hounds. Reassuringly, perhaps, not all of Somerset's doggie mirages are ominous.

We must not exclude Exmoor's celebrated ponies. The children's book illustrator and short fiction writer, the late Judy P. Powe, penned a nostalgic piece for the *West Somerset Reviewer* about the Moor's famous pony 'Tom'. 'It's an oft-told story, but knowing one or two well-known West Somerset folklorists, this was handed me down' she said. Here is the gist in the words of an old farmer, talking to a group of family youngsters:

In your grandfather's day, the pony herds were driven to Bampton Fair. Many were sold for pit ponies, and hundreds were sold or stolen for meat ... there were very few real Exmoor ponies left. That was when local farmers began to say they'd seen a wild pony stallion appear in the mist to lure the mares to safety. They called him 'Old Tom.'

Once, when we were trotting along the road, my pony snorted and looked towards a cut in the hillside. I crept to investigate. In the cut I saw a group of restless ponies. The mist had thickened, flowing into the combes, covering them in a white fleece. In the stillness I held my breath, waiting for something to happen. A proud stallion rose from the waterish veils, whickering softly, whiffling his nostrils, calling to the mares. The group clambered up the bank and vanished in the cloudish air. I had seen Exmoor's legendary ghost pony – Old Tom.

Stogursey's notorious Harriet the Witch is said to haunt the Witch Tree in the guise of a black dog. Huish Barton manor's black canine beastie was recorded in a letter by a departing resident in 1849. There have been many sightings by the manor staff, including one by the gardener. Weacombe, a tiny hamlet near the Quantocks is well known for its 'friendly' black dog, said to guide lost travellers along the country lanes.

Also, the writer Ruth Tongue remembered:

On Winsford Hill, on autumn nights a traveller may be stopped by a black hound with glowing saucer eyes. If he tries to advance he will die, either at once or very soon, but if he stands still

A friendly black dog guides lost travellers along this road at Weacombe.

Dancing bears have been sighted at The Shrubbery, Weston-super-Mare.

the dog will slowly vanish until only his eyes still glow. As soon as they disappear the traveller is free to move on, but some lesser ill-luck will follow. There was once a farmer whose frightened pony danced near to the spectre before he could stop it. The farmer did not die. It was the pony who collapsed half a mile from home.

Birds have always been venerated in ghost lore, and the belief that seeing a spirit bird denotes important changes in the home – even news foretelling a funeral. The claim that witches can shapeshift (the art of transforming into animal forms) into spirit animals, particularly cats and hares, is widely supported by various eye-witness accounts. In the 1920s a Combe Florey villager is on record as having regularly seen the 'spirit shades' of hares disappearing into trees or through old walls.

In 1994, a late night dogwalker, crossing Weston-super-Mare's Victorian park area, The Shrubbery, was puzzled and slightly frightened at the appearance of 'at least four' large black figures ambling and jumping in what is called 'the dip'. His dog began to growl and wrench at the lead. Deciding to avoid them, he back tracked to the road. Several days later, he described his encounter with an elderly resident, 'Some sees 'em, somes don't', she replied, adding 'They be bears. The big house down yonder kept bears, and when the land was fenced off, let them loose in a big pen. They still come back and play. My gran told me they were trained for circus dancing'.

Apparently, Margaret Cooper, residing in Ditcheat around 1580, saw what resembled a bear from the spirit world. It arrived in the upstairs room of her little cottage. Her screams woke her husband and brothers. Eventually, a local priest was called. He summoned it to appear. It did, and confronting the creature, and 'calling in the name of the Father, the Son and the Holy Ghost', it disappeared, never to be seen again. At the time, certain individuals thought it was the Devil, but the general view held that it was a ghost.

In the early 1600s, Richard Bovet's *Pandemonium or the Devil's Cloisters* noted that:

Mr. Edmund Ansty of South Petherton has occasion to return home by night from Woodbury Hill Fair, a mart well known in the West Country. Coming to a place not far from Yeovil noted by the name of Outhedge his horse rushed very violently with him against one side of the bank, snorting and trembling very much, so that he could by no means put him on his way, but he still pressed nearer to the bushes. At length Mr Ansty heard the hedges crack with a dismal noise and perceived coming towards him in the road which is there pretty wide a large circle of duskish light about the bigness of a very large wheel and in it he perfectly saw the proportion of a huge bear as clearly as if it had been by daylight. The spectre passed near him and as it came just over against the place where he was the monster looked very 'gushfully' at him showing a pair of very large flaming eyes. As soon as it was ever gone by, his horse sprung into the road and made homeward with so much haste that he could not possibly rein him in and had much ado to keep the saddle. There are many of the neighbours can witness the truth of it.

The images of black dogs are common throughout the UK. The Somerset poet C. Somerville Watson recalls that a phantom black dog with 'large fiery eyes' roamed a road in Beckington, 'with coat of black, and eyes of flame, that wander up and down the lane'.

Author Berta Lawrence gives credence to the phenomena surrounding Combwich:

At the Parrett end of a path between the Quantocks and Combwich ... in the shadow of Cynwit Castle the field-paths were long avoided after dark when the wild hunt might be encountered; the traveller would cower back and cover his face until the headless rider on his black horse and his demon pack of hounds with tongues of red flame, had swept by. They were seen even in the thick mist of an autumn dawn by a shepherd. To brush past the silent black ghost-dog who sometimes roamed at night, brought the worst luck of all.

Pixy Powers and Tree Spirits

A living, local 'conjuring man' believes that faeries and witches are 'one and the same'. This throws open an entirely new outlook on the role of pixie ghosties and the local wise woman or 'conjurer-man' (male witch). He said:

Trouble is, knowing if you're dealing with pixie ghosties or real little fellas. A witch has traffic with the faery realm, and I was told from old, that witches are also fairies, sometimes pixies, half-reborn into human form. It's why they're able to work with the faery folk.

Talking thus, we hear of Wiveliscombe's scarcely recorded ghost lore and what is reputed to be the chillingly haunted Park Wood, noted in 1911 for 'Old women on broomsticks with wraiths and goblins ...'

A faery dell.

At Maundown Top, we are told that within the last century, a charming stone cottage and an empty, mossy ruined farmhouse once stood. Rumours surrounded the vacant dwelling concerning various unpleasant events, including a blood-stained floor and the visitation by a very old long-bearded man, dressed in black velvet.

A poacher told the Rev. F. Hancock, Vicar of Dunster, that as he passed Tytibye's grave, the burial spot of a man called Tytibye that he saw a 'motionless figure' standing on the grave. Another tale tells of a young man who was hung near Maundown for murdering his mother. In time, his grinning skeletal remains and the gibbet fell to the ground, but his ghost continues to frequent the crossroads. The late vicar went out of his way to collect information about the haunting, together with extra gossip about pixie materializations. Of the murderer's spectral return:

> Still we hear that reputable people, as they draw near the place at night, see rising before them an indefinite but apparently tangible figure, which fills the roadway. Horses see it and become terrified. But as you approach it – if you are brave enough to do so, it gradually melts away.

Faery forms and pixies, have held faery gatherings at Cadbury Castle, where people confirm they have also seen the misty forms of Roman soldiers along the fortifications at full moon, their shields gleaming in the moonlight. Many well-attested glimpses of pixie-tree spirits throng the

Apple tree showing a pixie image.

pages of folk history. Trees were venerated, and scribes of yore mentioned 'dryads', or guardian tree souls. Throughout the world, numerous tribes and communities still uphold ceremonies to drive out unwanted spirits and call up the kindly ones.

Somerset is synonymous with the Apple Faery. It is believed that a robust wassail worship will conjure laden boughs. The word 'wassail' is from the Saxon 'Waes-heal', meaning 'good health.' Carhampton hosts one of the most popular wassails, held behind the Butcher's Arms in January. Many private garden wassails are still held throughout the county today. The wrinkly bark faces seen in many trees, particularly the oak, apple, elm and elder, are thought to be the images of pixie ghosts.

The Nurses

Discussions with nurses from Weston-super-Mare general hospital and Taunton's Musgrove evoked reminiscences of a childhood admittance to the renowned Canadian Memorial Red Cross Hospital in land adjacent to the Clivedon estate, Buckinghamshire. I was transferred to the men's surgical ward, due to the children's ward being full. On four consecutive nights, a middle-aged nurse used to visit several of the beds, stooping over the sleeping patients then fading into the low-lit atmosphere. Nurse 'E', put it down to 'dreams'. Some years later, an artist and acquaintance of the Astors corroborated these experiences, 'Very true, very true, there are numerous sightings of more than one spirit nurse on the wards, but, they are very kind and friendly'. The nurses at Weston and Taunton spoke of figures and footsteps along several of the wards.

Halsway Manor.

Secrets of Halsway

Imposing its upslope architectural Tudor finery, Halsway Manor exudes a serene and graceful setting, surrounded seasonally by sprigs and sprays of colourful gardens. 'Halsway' means 'pass road', as the cottages and manor huddle between two hills. The manor is recorded in the *Domesday Book*. Today, it is the thriving National Centre for Traditional Music, Dance and Song, offering a lively programme of regular meetings, embracing the West Somerset Morris Men, Halsway Folk Dance Group and a year-long list of lectures, recitals, craft fairs and other musical feasts.

Members of the English Folk Dance and Song Society purchased Halsway in 1965, and it currently provides beds for up to sixty-two people. Just how many visitors have seen its ghosts is speculative, but many folk say they have. Halsway's Cliff Branson confirmed reports about 'the lady on the stairs … apparently Room 15'.

A Candle in the Window

We have heard tell in a mid-Somerset hamlet that, 'A witch is a witch is a witch. All colours good and bad.' We may have also heard, 'There's no more venom in a ghost than the ghost of a black witch'. Fortunately, there is an increasing enlightenment about the witch and her counterpart, the conjure or cunning-man. Granted there were certain unpleasant exceptions to the rule, but the village 'wise ones' were mostly healers, offering kindly understanding to birds, beasts and humans. However, representing the Old Nature Religion, its gods and elemental influences, they were seen by many Christian sects as a threat to the spread of Churchianity. Among the still many unknowns about witches and their 'craft' is the subject of ghosts. There are many recorded examples of witches being called to perform 'secret rites' to disperse a restless spirit or quell an angry ghost.

The traditional witch, only too aware that there are 'two sides to every coin' knew how to employ 'reverse magic' to protect against unwanted ghosts, or 'see them off'; hence the use of talismans, lucky charms and 'drawing lights'. The latter came with the advent of the candle, which gradually replaced rushlights. A candle set in the window was a common practice to 'draw good spirits'.

Somerset brims with ghostly witches. Another witchy ability, was the use of an astrological almanac to aid an understanding of whatever may be afflicting a troubled individual or location. The cultural historian Owen Davies notes:

> At the inquest on the body of Mary Saunders of Lufton, Somerset, in June 1892, it was stated that, believing their daughter to have been bewitched, her parents visited the South Petherton cunning man, James Stacey. The father of the deceased told the coroner: 'I told him (Stacey) I did not know whether there was any such spell over her. He said he would look on the almanack, and then said no-one could "overlook" her, because she was the first born child.' It would seem then, that almanacks were used on different levels depending on the interests and sophistication of the reader.

Banishing or scaring off ghosts has worldwide parallels, exampled by the Roman Festival of Manes, designed to appease wandering ghosts. Likewise, China's Hungry Ghosts celebration during August, had similar aims.

One method of preventing the ghosts of witches 'returning from the dead' was to bury them north in the churchyard, or more preferably at a crossroads; likewise were suicides, which is said to explain the large number of crossroad hauntings. Perhaps many of the sightings of ghostly hares, dogs and even birds, are none other than witches shapeshifting – perhaps so that they may roam freely to keep an eye on the locals?

Spirits of Sedgemoor

The patch of ground at a crossroads between Stogumber and Crowcombe is not for the squeamish say devotees of the unexplained. Much to the consternation of Stogumber and Crowcombe people, the huge Heddon Oak was felled in the 1980s, as it was deemed unsafe. Long before it was axed, Minehead's book illustrator Judy P. Powe drew its massive boughs, an icon of numerous great trees throughout the county where hundreds of tortured corpses of hung rebels swung in all weathers – a reminder of the Battle of Sedgemoor's bloody carnage, on 6 July 1685. It was the last battle to be fought on English soil, and although estimates vary, it is claimed that over 1,000 men gave their lives for a proverbial lost cause.

Heddon Oak's ominous ambience is legendary, and the three hanged rebels, George Gillard, John Lockstone and Arthur Williams were its victims. The October 2006 *Westonzoyland Parish Magazine* carries this compelling item by Cathy Bryon-Edmond of Sedgemoor Tourism about the Battle of Sedgemoor Trail, 'The project to develop an exciting new interpretive trail based on the Battle of Sedgemoor is nearing completion … plans are being finalised to install the series

Right: *A typical Somerset gallows oak.*

Below: *Sedgemoor battle site.*

Above: *Sedgemoor memorial.*

Left: *Sedgemoor's guardian trees.*

Westonzoyland church.

of signs, way marker posts and panels'. Either side of Westonzoyland's Battle of Sedgemoor's monument, grow two lofty trees. Like sentinel pillars, these white poplars are enshrined in tree lore as symbols of life and death, appropriate icons for a memorial to those who fought and died on both sides.

The conflict began when James I, a Roman Catholic, came to the throne in 1685. He was immediately challenged by his nephew, the Duke of Monmouth from Holland, who led a West Country rebellion, drawing his armed forces from across Somerset. Trapped in Bridgwater by the Royal Army, commanded by Lord Faversham and Lord Churchill, Monmouth's army of poorly armed peasant folk were no match for the King's highly trained troops. The chaos which followed the muddled tactics of Monmouth's outnumbered rebels led to a bloodbath, and in a locally published pamphlet for visitors, the historian Maurice Page wrote:

> The Royal troops disgraced themselves by indiscriminate slaughter of the beaten rebels, many of whom were shot or hanged in cold blood. About five hundred prisoners were herded into Westonzoyland church, where they were kept alive until the Bloody Assize. Five of them died of their wounds in the church.
>
> An entry in the parish register says 'The battle began between one and two of the clock in the morning. It continued nearly one hour and a halfe'.

List of convicted rebels.

One of the church wardens recorded the immediate hanging of several rebels, and that sixteen of the king's men were buried either in the church or the churchyard. When the prisoners were finally released, a large amount of frankincense, pitch, saltpetre and resin was used to fumigate Sedgemoor's Parish church of St Mary the Virgin.

More than 1,000 rebels were buried in deep pits, and the modern memorial is said to mark the place of the heaviest fighting. Try to imagine the sheer horror of it all. Even the most hardened sceptics have admitted to the overpowering sense of foreboding that pervades this bleakly inhospitable area.

Bridgwater-born Dr Barry Moyse told of a haunting at the Rose and Crown in St Mary Street, of disembodied footsteps in the night, which some say are those of a rebel who was allegedly hung from the inn's sign. Sometimes the roll of thunder is heard even when the sky is crystal clear, perhaps a memory of distant military drums.

Returning to the subject of the many hanging trees, said to trigger unusual disturbances – people living in the vicinity of the battlefield also believe they have heard horses in full gallop and the moans of fallen soldiers. Others interviewed talk of the White Lady, who tends the Sedgemoor Memorial site.

To apply a pun, author Alan L. Holt 'makes no bones' about listing the number of executed by the 'Bloody' Judge Jeffreys. They belonged:

> … to at least thirty-four towns and villages in Somerset. The number of those whom Judge Jeffreys assigned to be hanged, drawn and quartered and the places in Somerset where the hangings took place are as follows: Axbridge 6; Bridgwater 9; Bruton 3; Castle Cary 3; Chard 12; Chewton Mendip 2; Crewkerne 10; Cothelstone 2; Dunster 3; Dulverton 3; Frome 12; Glastonbury 5; Ilchester 12; Ilminster 12; Langport 3; Milborne Port 2; Minehead 6; Nether Stowey 3; Norton St Philip 13; Porlock 2; Shepton Mallet 12; Somerton 7; Stogursey 2; Taunton 19; Wellington 3; Wells 8; Wincanton 7; Wiveliscombe 3; and Yeovil 7.

*Sedgemoor
memorial stone.*

Among the numerous accounts of 'Sedgemoor spirits' is an occurrence at Clayton's Corner Crossroads, on the Bridgwater-Stogursey road, and the appearance of a soldier from the battlefield. A 250-year-old ghost! Some twenty or so years ago, Somerset County Council workmen, replacing the worn signpost, dug up the bones of a man clothed in a red uniform. He was thought to have been hanged at the crossroads as a deserter.

Fugitives from the conflict are reported to haunt a place near a cluster of elm trees. A man named King Starr advised them to hide in a mow of wheat on the lynch. Under threat from the pursuing troops, Starr revealed their hiding place. They were flushed out and hanged on an elm tree. Interestingly, the name King Starr is in the local register book for 1753. The battlefield apparition of the Lord of Locking Manor reminds of his untimely death after the battle. John Plumley, who had joined Monmouth's army, fled and hid in a place, still known as Plumley's Coppice. His dog, running out of the coppice, sadly betrayed his master's whereabouts. Plumley was later hanged.

Fair Rosamund

Another, little known spinoff to Heddon's history, and probably other such crossroads hauntings arose during a conversation with an elderly 'conjuring man' whose family roots feed richly in Exmoor traditions. He said that in many areas adherents of the Old Faith had their own version of the goddess 'Diana worship'. However, he said, most of Somerset's Old Religion followed 'Rosimundi' (Rose of the World), or 'Fair Rosamund'. He said, 'Cross roads are the four sacred quarters, North, South, East and West … yur at the centre of everything when yur in the midst of everything … fact folk were hanged there, deters strangers, so we can get on with our work'.

Perhaps the story of Fair Rosamund a young girl with golden hair, who it was said, was the sweetheart of Henry II, seen gliding behind the high reinforced walls surrounding Cannington Priory, is a secret reference to the area being a former place of pagan goddess worship.

The Danish Boy

The late Berta Lawrence, considered among the finest writers on the county's history, notes in *Quantock Country*:

> Near Danesborough Ring the Quantock woodmen swore they heard ghostly music issuing from underground, the revelling of Viking warriors feasting with wassail-cup and song. Another story tells of Danish marauders who, after seizing Quantock women, were lured to their death at the hands of Quantock men – except one fair-haired boy, hidden and saved by a woman who loved him. The ghostly Danish boy was supposed to wander the wooded slopes of Danesborough …

Other Haunts

If you enjoy browsing through bookshops, you may on more than one occasion find yourself confronted by an abundance of ghost books. And that, in the proverbial nutshell, is what this book has so far been about; pulling together a wide range of psychic, supernatural and unexplained events with fresh angles on the old, in tandem with unpublished material.

When, or if you meet a ghost, you mostly partake of history because most ghostly occurrences tend to engrave a partially visible memory, possibly embedded in a kind of magnetic broadband of a yesteryear episode or major historic incident. Many of these unreal realities are enduring and persistent, and in their visitations are often locked challenging secrets. So, before we journey on, here are some briefer snippets, written up or by word of mouth from around some of the county's delightful villages.

Described as a finer poet than writer, making the acquaintance of Stogumber's late Richard Elmes was always fertile when it came to the topic of short stories, for which Richard employed a keen typewriter. He did confirm that there were many mysterious legends surrounding the village. Stogumber, below the Brendons, is a gorgeous cluster of various, tipply-topply dwellings, and is worth visiting to enjoy its colourful angles, stones and bricks and quaint windows. The village flows down the side of the hill to a mineral spring. Also, near the railway station, is a 'faery well'. And as if to echo the countryside's pixie traditions, a pillar near the altar of the robust dignity of Stogumber's St Mary, ('A large and ambitious church,' said Nikolaus Pevsner) defines a cheerfully faced Jack-in-the-Green, encircled by leaves.

Then there is the Blood Field, above the former Heddon Oak, scene of a gory battle between the Britons and Saxons. In 1957, William Chidley recalled a pine tree with iron spikes jutting from its trunk, believed to have been used as a gallows tree to execute captives from a violent battle there, linked to Sedgemoor's Monmouth rebellion – so violent, that the field was covered in blood and scattered human limbs.

Publicly, Richard Elmes was usually guarded about many 'psychical things,' but privately, gave credit to the doubt. Interestingly, he lived not far from the village, which brags several strange tales and none more telling than those who say they have either seen or heard of 'folks who've heard' about the thunderous beat of hooves in tandem with weird lights and half-formed riders, as the demonic horsemen of a wild hunt gallops through Stogumber's streets. It is said to be championed by the god, Woden himself, leading the large company of beings and beasts. This awesome spectacle is said to have been last seen during the 1960s. It is held to be extremely unlucky to those who see the vision.

Stogumber – scene of the wild hunt.

By considerable contrast, the Religious Society of Friends (Quakers) tend to scarcity when it comes to ghosts. Milverton Friends' burial ground is occasionally revisited by a figure wearing traditional Quaker attire.

Cloaked figures are said to move across the hallway of Banwell Abbey, and a white lady visits King John's Hunting Lodge at Axbridge. Also, a spirit cat makes an appearance.

Bicknoller

Whether you accept, disbelieve or prefer open mindedness, certain Bicknoller residents have disclosed making unexpected contact with 'the other side'. However, the contemplative tranquillity of Bicknoller's walks and lanes seem ghost free, though a number of locals will tell you that 'they've been seen, but so quick as not to say what they're like'.

Bicknoller has attracted much literary and artistic attention. Somerset's revered historian, Collinson, admired its ancient yew, and over a century ago, the writer Richard Jefferies praised the area's serenity and spirit of antiquity. And then there's a tale about a faery coach, a figure wearing silk and a black dog, which either romps the hill path or decides to reappear along the Weacombe road.

Blackdown Hills

The Blackdown Hills are reputedly as haunted as the Quantocks, and even today, some of the locals think thrice before setting out late at night. Rumour has it that the span of road at Hillyhead, which passes a cemetery, is extremely sinister. The Blackdowns are also said to be faery haunted, as these extracts from Thomas Keightley's *Fairy Mythology,* reveal:

> The place near which they (the faeries) most ordinarily showed themselves was on the side of a hill, named Blackdown … not many miles from Taunton … appearing like men and women, of a stature generally nearer the smaller size of men. Their habits used to be of red, blue, or green, according to the old way of country garb, with high crowned hats …

Two 'faery songs' were sung to the late folklorist Ruth Tongue by a local resident, 'Annie's Granny' in 1922. Here's the first verse of 'The Spunky':

> The Spunky he went like a sad little flame,
> All, all alone,
> All out on the zogs (marshland) and a-down the lane,
> All, all alone.
> A tinker came by that was full of ale,
> And into the mud he went head over tail,
> All, all alone.

A 'spunky' is a will-o-the-wisp, which is said to be the spirit of an unbaptised child enticing travellers to marshlands, hopeful that they will christen it so that it may join the Christian souls in church. Turnip lanterns lit at Halloween are called punkies.

Buried Treasure

Robin Hood's Butts (Brow Moor), or similarly named places, refer to 'Robin' as the Green God of Nature. 'Hood' refers to the hood, worn by Woden, or 'Grim', venerated widely by Saxon Somerset. Over the centuries, pagan devotees have, when possible, continued to use the age-old stone circles for their worship and meetings. A fascinating legend emerges, and one not uncommon to many such places – buried treasure. Pirates and smugglers aside, gold pieces-of-eight and hoards of great antiquity are believed to have been hidden away in Somerset soil, caves and other unlikely places. Here is another variation of a Blackdown hills tradition:

> I was one of the workman hired to find a big gold burial at Old Robin's place, and I tell you this, twas' a terrible situation for all of us.' T. was one of at least ten workmen, employed by a 'man-o-means' to dig it up, an I was the only one to fear what might happen. T. had been warned about digging up one of the two large round barrows. He told the rich man and the other men that these ancient graves were alleged to be defended by 'overseeing spirits'.

The diggers laboured long and hard, removing huge swathes of earth and propping up the ditch with large posts. Worryingly, they did not seem to be making much progress, because the barrows remained more or less the same as when they started. A frustrating day passed and the men returned home. At next dawn they were baffled to see that the posts had been removed and the ditches covered with gorse and grass. The men left in a panic. However, not to be daunted, the wealthy man angrily picked up a spade and began digging. After some hours, he stood to survey his efforts, but to his amazement, everything had returned the same as he first found it. No one has ever uncovered the buried treasure.

Parallel legends of concealed or lost treasure occur throughout the UK, and their folklore unveils a similar truth, that guardian ghosts or other paranormal activists seem to work against whoever attempts to release their riddles.

The Creech Hill Fiend

Everyone relishes a 'whatever is in that dark cupboard' tale. Ghosts love sceptics. In fact, the 'I don't believe in them' is definitely teasing fate. That was exactly what happened, or so the account goes, to a sceptical Bruton farmer in the late 1800s, trudging home from market as night's veils began to fall.

The road and certain areas around the massive, eccentric contours of Creech Hill had already gained a dark name for unworldly horrors – in the shape of a fiendish figure. The farmer had doubtless heard of a Bruton resident's recent terrifying encounter, crossing the hill by lantern light. Cackling laughter filled his ears as something seemed to physically impede his progress. He fainted and was found by two farm workers the next day. Needless to add, he was ill for several weeks. The farm men confirmed that they had heard of the 'fiend'.

Continuing his journey, our Bruton farmer saw a figure crouching in the road. Thinking he or she was ill or had been injured, he approached, offering help. Whatever it was, the figure leaped up screeching. The farmer fled, but the fiendish shape ran after him. Reaching his farmhouse, he burst through the door and fell traumatised to the floor. His startled wife and children ran outside to confront the attacker, only to see a tall black figure laughing and shrieking as it shambled back in the direction of Creech Hill. This macabre character still appears today, together with the sound of heavy footsteps and a feeling of frosty coldness.

Haunting Bridgwater

Beautiful Bridgwater, bathed in one of those powdery Somerset twilights, mirrors plenty of historical gems. Its most celebrated citizen, Admiral Robert Blake, baptised in 1599, was esteemed for his valiant leadership at sea. Tony James in his recent book *Yankee Jack Sails Again* sums it up:

> You must walk along West Quay and turn up from the river into Castle Street for perhaps the richest reward for visiting Bridgwater – a tiny and totally unexpected wonderland of exquisite Georgian and Regency architecture regarded by English Heritage as perhaps the finest in the West Country. Standing guard at the top of nearby Cornhill is F.W. Pomeroy's bronze statue of Bridgwater's most famous son, Sir Robert Blake, Cromwell's favourite Admiral, who won more naval battles than Nelson. Not bad for someone who was originally in the army and scorned port and starboard in favour of 'left and right'.

Statue of Admiral Blake.

Blake was educated at the local grammar school and in the marketplace, his austere but noble statue still venerates his service to the nation. In spite of little evidence, there are those who are convinced that he still frequents his birthplace.

It is unimaginable that such a robust personality could fail to have left some psychic trace of his life. Like Lord Nelson, Blake was the epitome of the British spirit's formidable fortitude against all adversity. Blake's presence is said to be 'felt' in his house, now the Blake Museum of tribute to his seafaring courage.

There are scant but findable remains of Bridgwater Castle, built in 1216, founded on the present King's Square site, including the 700-year-old stone archway. If Bridgwater is the 'capital of the moors', then her superlative parish church, St Mary is a sacred capital for townspeople and visitors alike. The church has a marvellous collection of screens and fine carvings. At least one 'ghostly worshipper' has been seen among the pews. And are the mysterious cloak-clad figures of Silver Street's arched doorway of the 1220s a throwback to Grey Friars' monks?

Hide-and-Seek

Ghostly gossip reports of a potentially frightening encounter with a phantom coach and horses on the Bridgwater to Pawlett road. Continuing to nearby Bawdrip, another restless soul supposedly lingers mournfully in the vicinity of the thirteenth-century St Michael's and All Angels Parish church.

The Blake Museum.

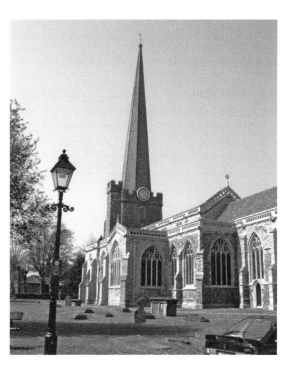

Bridgwater Parish church.

Bawdrip – St Michael and All Angels.

Does pretty Eleanor Lovell still search in vain? On a bright, sunny 14 June 1681, following her wedding, Eleanor and younger guests decided on a game of hide-and-seek. Traditionally, this old game can be quite scary, depending on who leaps out on whom, when and where. But this particular and well-recorded game of hide-and-seek could match even the most hideous of nightmarish plots.

It was hoped to be one of Eleanor's wedding highlights, something for the youngsters to laugh about and remember, a sort of 'party piece' to conclude a day the like of which Bawdrip had never seen before; the aftermath of a day when bells peeled, and footmen and gorgeously dressed bridesmaids adorned the event. According to memories passed down, the villagers danced, sang folk songs and enjoyed all kinds of merriment. Young Eleanor was adored by everyone.

Hunting out a hiding place was a challenge. Eventually, Eleanor entered the rectory, with its narrow corridors and many rooms. Half hidden in a niche of an empty room, she discovered an age-worn oaken chest. She opened the weighty lid. It would be a tight squeeze, but it was the perfect place to disappear from the distant laughter and whoops of her young friends, already starting to seek her out. A very tight squeeze, she gently lowered the weighty lid.

After some time, Eleanor thought it best to clamber out. She could not lift the heavy lid. The thick oak chest would have trapped her calls and screams for help. A desperate search by her panic-stricken husband, together with family, friends and others revealed no trace of Eleanor. After many days, weeks and months, and countless rumours, Eleanor was given up as 'lost' or 'dead'. She was dead; suffocated in that oak-tomb chest.

The Old Rectory, Bawdrip, where a game of hide-and-seek ended in tragedy.

Several years later, a local man came across the chest. With considerable effort and curiosity, he raised its heavy lid. The shock must have been horrific. Still wearing her now discoloured but glamorous wedding dress, were the gruesome, half-skeletal remains of Eleanor Lovell. Her

Legend links her with claims that her choking cries haunt the stillness of summer nights. Her untimely tragedy has been remembered by Somerset writer Haynes Bayley's poem *The Mistletoe Bough*. Also, a play by Charles Somerset *The Fatal Chest* was staged at London's Garrick Theatre in 1834.

Fiddington's Phantoms

Not only does the charming church, dedicated to St Martin of Tours, in the West Somerset village of Fiddington, display several fine examples of carved-oak bench ends, but also, outside and partially obscured by centuries of weathering, there stands a remnant of old paganism. Near the main entrance, high on the wall, crudely incised in stone is a strange figure. Its head is round with bulging eyes. The left arm raised, while the right arm rests on the right knee.

The 'idol' is usually recognised as a sheela-na-gig, from the Irish gaelic, or 'sighle-na-gcioch' translated as 'Julia' or 'Celia of the Breasts'. They mark out pagan sites of worship. There are at least twenty samples of the sheela-na-gig in England and seventy in Ireland.

The Sheela-na-gig carved in the stonework at Fiddington church.

As Earth Goddess, her display of female power was said to have symbolised powerful magic against negative spiritual forces. These heathen powers are thought to have been incorporated in church decoration to maintain the attendance of congregations who were still largely pagan. Floating lights, shadowy shapes and even a walking figure have been seen from time to time to the west area of the burial ground. Are they imaged echoes of pagan worship in this area ... the old believers still returning to remind us of their timeless allegiance to the old gods?

Tap, Tap, Tap

A Mr H. Spicer in 1864 wrote that in an old house near Frome:

> ... on almost every night, at twelve o'clock, something that was invisible entered a certain corridor at one end, and passed out at the other ... Almost as regularly as night succeeded day, the strange sound recurred, and was precisely that which would have been occasioned by a lady, wearing the high-heeled shoes of a former period, and a full silk dress, sweeping through the corridor. Nothing was ever *seen* – and the impression produced by hearing the approach, the passing, and withdrawal of the visitor with perfect distinctness, while the companion-sense was shut, was described as most extraordinary.

He continued to describe how friends of his brother decided to wait up and confront the invisible visitor, and sure enough, they too heard the tapping footsteps and the swirl of a rustling dress. During a discussion about their unseen visitor, one of his friends remarked:

> I may mention that, on one occasion, it chanced that a nurse in the family had to pass through the corridor about the hour of twelve, carrying, or rather leading, a little girl *who was deaf and dumb*. As the sounds passed, the child appeared to shrink back in utmost alarm, struggling

and moaning to get away, nor could she ever be induced to enter the corridor again, without evincing the same violent terror.

Haunted Holford

Below fiery gorse and purple heather of the emerald-leaved heights of the Quantocks, narrow snaking lanes wind to haunted Holford Glen. 'Pixie haunted' as Arthur L. Salmon notes in his *Literary Rambles in the West of England*:

> The pixie is the special Celtic variant of the ordinary faery or elf, and it only lingers now in the West of England. Its chief homes are on Dartmoor and in Cornwall, but its presence on Exmoor and among the Quantocks proves a similar continuance of Celtic tradition … Within living memory a farmer is said to have seen some threshing his corn, in a barn near Holford village. Unhappily, he shouted his approval of their industry, which, like true West Somerset pixies, they resented so strongly that they vanished and have never been seen since.

This theme of pixies threshing corn is widespread, and it has been said that in some instances they are the wraiths of the 'little fellas', long passed on. Nevertheless, where freshly threshed corn has been discovered, there seems to be only one answer —labours of love by living pixie folk!

Writing and researching during the 1920s, writer Mrs A.C. Osborn Hann would have treasured the then available knowledge of the county's folklore, especially the numerous sitings of ghosts and tales of impish faery folk or the quaintly wise sayings of folk magic, 'There is one moment when dusk ends and evening begins when, if you make a wish, "They" will grant it'. It is also believed that at this twinkle between dusk and nightfall, the spirit world is closer to the world of human affairs.

Holford's Plough Inn dates to the Elizabethan calendar. Holford is given in the *Domesday Book* under 'Hulofort' and 'Holeford'. Nestled beneath great swathes of wood-lushed hills and winding woodland paths, the Plough is imprinted with the comings and goings of human appetites and wander-weary travellers. However, there is one character who, for whatever reason, has become a permanent resident. He has been called 'The Spanish Traveller', though some believe he was involved in politics, which in 1555 could be dangerous. Mary Tudor was on the throne during a period of heightened tension between England and Spain. Also, there was widespread public and political disapproval of her marriage to the King of Spain. Whichever side of this startling morsel you choose, remember that the main ingredients do not change. Most folk opt for report 'No.1':

> Journeying to Bristol, a wealthy Spanish merchant booked an overnight stay at the inn. With time to spare, he joined in the chit chat and probably even went as far to buy a 'couple of rounds'. It became evident that he was carrying a goodly sum of gold coins. Later, as he trod the outside stone steps to his bedroom, he was attacked and killed. The robber or robbers broke into his bedroom to steal his hoard, but found nothing.

The alternative sequence of events describes how he was strangled while he slept. Once again, the murderous hands never found the gold. Centuries since, he has been haunting the inn, albeit a friendly spirit. The stone steps have long gone, but there are those who say that they have heard his footfall climbing the steps. One customer has even seen his faint outline by the open fireplace. Perhaps the Spaniard periodically returns to look for his hidden gold?

The fireplace at Holford's Plough Inn.

Langport's Black Dog

Called the 'Thomas Hardy of Somerset', that ominously forgotten novelist and playwright Walter Raymond might have been cautious of ghosts, yet many of his novels include folkloric themes. Unfortunately, his books and other writings are now hard to find.

Walter, who died at Southampton on 2 April 1931, was the son of a Yeovil glove manufacturer, Cuthbert Raymond. He also spent sixteen years of his life in a modest Withypool cottage. Among his many books, Raymond mentions the famous 'Black Dog of Langport'. In his enchanting *Tryphena in Love* the first verses read:

> The black dog o'Langport have-a-burned off his tail,
> And this is the night of our jolly Wassail.

It is thought that this winter festive song refers to the Devil having been singed by all the seasonal goodwill. Furthermore, this same black dog, mentioned in so many county hauntings could, according to J.L. Page in his *Exploration of Dartmoor*, be one of the packs of 'wish' or 'yeth' hounds which return to alarm unwary travellers crossing Exmoor and Dartmoor. Mr Page mentions that a coach driver, crossing the moor in daylight exclaimed in front of his passengers, 'There! There! Do you see *that?*', pointing out a large black dog running alongside the coach, '…it is the black dog that hunts the Moor!' This also raises the question, are some of the sightings of the legendary Beast of Exmoor none other than a 'wish hound'?

Malignant Spirit

The death of the Benedictine monk Dom Petit Pierre saw the passing of one of the last great exorcists. During a personal interview before Nashdom Abbey's Holy Order, relocated to Prinknash, we met, and under a summer's spreading cedar tree in the abbey's meditative peace, Dom Petit made listening both fascinating and mysterious:

> Naturally, I believe in ghosts, or if you prefer, lost souls, or simply image-memories, because it is my work, from time to time, to, as it were, exorcise … help those who in some way need the strength of compassionate prayer. And, yes, of course, there are challenging spirits, shall we say, naughty ones!? Through the rites of exorcism we 'lay' or ease the journey of the 'straying' departed.

This takes us to Wellington and the nitty gritties of sorting out the unsorted spirit in a house in Fore Street. It was the former home of a banker, of whom hardly a good word could be said. Many Wellington people believe to this day that he must have been a rascally character because his ghostly occupation of the house created havoc. His spirit was claimed to be malignant, in that items were thrown about; there were shouts, curses and on one occasion, a terrifying appearance. A successful exorcism was performed with the efforts of the then local vicar and the Baptist minister.

The Creaking

Separating the facts from the fiction of Jack White's Gibbet has been daunting for ghoul hunters, let alone historians of sensational murder cases. The difference between execution by gibbet and hanging was that the convicted felon was first hanged, then his body taken to a crossroads '…to expose the dead body of a malefactor when the court could lawfully add that ignomy to the capital sentence'. *(Encyclopaedia of the Laws of England, 1898)*

However, if we are to believe what happened to Jack White, then his gibbeting was truly inhumane, and many believe, unjustified. It is the perfect scenario for the return of an anguished, restless spirit. In fact, it was a controversial move on the part of the county judiciary to sentence a criminal to be hung in chains at the place of murder. The crossway where the main road between Wincanton and Castle Cary overlaps is where Jack White's body was hung out to decay and to be a warning to other would-be rogues. It is still extremely haunted.

The most factual report of Jack White's trial, gibbeting and reports of psychic disturbances may be studied in the many issues of the *Castle Cary Visitor* (1896–1915). The crime formed the basis of numerous ballads, poems and even plays, including Walter Raymond's *No Soul above Money*.

John (Jack) White was a Wincanton boy who 'got in the wrong company' and inevitably was in and out of trouble, usually through drunkenness, spending much of his earnings from occasional work at various inns – his favourite being the Sun. In spite of everything, he married, at twenty-six, a 'devoted and loyal' wife, Sarah Slade, and enjoyed fourteen happy years.

It was at the Sun that Jack White met Robert Sutton, a messenger, carrying a valuable document for a 'local gentleman'. For whatever reasons, several drunken arguments ensued, but Sutton decided that the delivery of the document was more important than risking brawls and asked Jack to guide him to the address. According to the evidence before Mr Baron Thompson at Bridgwater Assizes, 6 August 1730, Jack White was quite intoxicated when the two men encountered two women. Jack accosted one of them with a kiss. His attempt to flirt with the second woman was angrily resisted. Sutton intervened. They quarrelled. The women left. Sutton, trying to calm White, offered him a half guinea to complete the journey.

Much the wose for drink, the pair rested at the crossroads for Holton, Bratton and Castle Cary. White, still angry and inebriated, and in his own public confession said, 'When through drunkenness, and the Devil's Suggestion, I embrew'd my Hand in his innocent Blood, for which I beg heartily the Forgiveness of God'. It was, to all reports, a nasty murder. Jack White had 'beat out' one of Sutton's eyes, 'ran a stick in at his mouth and out through the neck, and otherwise mangled his victim.'

The 1922's edition of *The Somerset Year Book* read, 'Although there is no evidence that punishment by starvation was ever the law in this country, the story of Jack White being left to starve in his cage at the well-know crossroads now bearing his name is still firmly believed by many ...' Curiously, a while after White's execution, that renowned, reliable Castle Cary diarist, Squire Woodforde, declared to friends during an evening dinner that he was not afraid to speak to the corpse. Walking past the gibbet on his return home, he reportedly asked the suspended corpse, 'Well, Jack, how be you?' To his shock, the corpse hissed, 'Jack's cold, turble cold!' This raises the theory that White might not have been executed, but left to starve and decompose to the elements and hungry crows. Some claim that the ghosts of Jack White and Robert Sutton regularly disturb the area. Many still imagine they hear the creaking of the gibbet during the day and night.

Other Entities

This final chapter is intended as a wider trawl of the many hearsays, observations and notes from an array of sources; a mix and mingle for those who plan to explore Somerset's ghost spots.

The poet Samuel Taylor Coleridge, who lived in West Somerset for a few years, was famed for *The Rime of the Ancient Mariner*, which local tradition claims to have been written at the ancient seaport of Watchet. In one of his poems, Coleridge reflects on a deserted, rubbled castle, overgrown by vines and a symphony of nightingales. He may have meant the now deserted site of Stowey Castle, which even today has a reputation for unidentified manifestations.

There is a tradition of hauntings linked to the giants of Nether Stowey; noisy thuds and moans from the tumuli close to the town. There are similar tales of the same giants, terrorising the people of Stogursey. Eventually, according to a Quantock saying, 'Men from Dowsboro' beat down Stowey Castle, and men from Stogursey beat down Stogursey Castle' and slew the huge invaders. This is reveried in similar countrywide folk tales of giants overcome by the local population, including the famous *Jack the Giant Killer* faery tale.

Many curious beliefs surround disembodied spirits and other astral ambiences. It is commonly believed that a change in the mood or temperature of a building, place or area can denote the presence of netherworld phenomena. This isn't always the fact because numerous individuals claim they have had little or no warning whatsoever. Things just happen.

Joan Carne, Peggy Parsons and The Witch Hare

The late Exmoor journalist Jack Hurley, who in his *Legends of Exmoor* gave many ghostly yarns a mainly tongue-in-cheek review, was however clever enough to keep an open mind. Jack was only too well aware that the imagination can play havoc, especially when walking or motoring through dark wooded places.

So much has been written and guessed about secluded Withycombe's Sandhill Manor and Madam Joan Carne that peeling the facts from the inventions would test the news-craft of even the most painstaking of noses for news. Jack wrote:

> The lady is exceptionally good value. In addition to giving the run around as a hare, she is an upper class witch, a suspected disposer of one or more husbands and she comes back to Sandhill after her own funeral to fry eggs and bacon. This is a bonus legend indeed!

In 1573 a Taunton man, John Newton, married Joan, who had come from Dunster. After his death, she married Charles Wyndham of Williton's Orchard Wyndham lineage. He died in 1585. Joan then married Thomas Carne of Glamorgan, taking his name for which she became known, Madam Joan Carne.

There have been repeated and unsuccessful attempts to exorcise Madam Carne's ghost, and earliest accounts say that she was banished into the nearby 'Witch's Pool' but still manages to return and haunt her former home. At her death and owing to her witchy reputation, Madam Carne's coffin was sealed with iron nails. Mourners returning to Sandhill Manor were horrified to witness Joan frying eggs and bacon. A nearby priest was summoned and succeeded in temporarily driving her phantasm into the pond.

Living several years at one of Somerset's 'queen of resorts', ghosts and their kin proved unavoidable. Peggy Parsons, who resided near Sand Bay, might not be a match for Mother Leakey or Joan Carne, but Peggy possessed a formidable and kindly reputation as local wise woman. Numbers of people claim to have seen her wandering along the Kewstoke Road close to the former tollgate, and others have caught glimpses of her walking among the shadows of Weston Woods, near Picwinna's or Picwinard's Mound (also called Peak Winnard). This comes as no revelation because Picwinna has for centuries been thrown together by stones and pebbles, gathered and carried to be cast by local fisherfolk and people who believe in its wish-bringing powers. Ill-luck is reputed to fall on anyone who removes one of the stones. When throwing a stone, a little rhyme was chanted, 'Picwinna, picwinna, Pick me some dinner'.

Elsewhere, there was gossip concerning an unnamed local witch, whose deeds are recalled by a correspondent, Mr W. F. Rose, writing in 1875. A farmer in Worle blamed the sudden death of his pigs on an older local suspect, and a warlock from Taunton was contacted who eventually identified her from several accused women:

> It was perhaps, unfortunate that the poor old woman who bore the worst repute in all such matters should have come to an untimely end – through falling into the fire on her hearth. It must be added that, on the morning of this sad event, the harriers on the adjacent hill lost their hare among some stone walls, where it was next day picked up dead. The man who found it,

Kewstoke Toll Road – said to be frequented by the ghost of Peggy Parsons.

Picwinna's Mound – Weston-super-Mare.

took it to his master's house, but on his bringing it into the kitchen, the maids immediately rushed out in terror and wouldn't 'bide' in the house with it, declaring that it was old Mrs – .

It is a common belief that witches have the power of transforming themselves into hares, though in this case it is hard to see what advantage would have accrued through so doing, but I suppose there was a vague sort of idea that the witch and her double had passed away at the same moment.

Even so, the place where it all happened, not far from Sand Bay, is said to remain haunted.

The Vanishing

Can places disappear and then reappear? The author and journalist Jon Dathen tells of an extraordinary car journey to Wookey Hole, on a road which follows the valley of the River Axe. Jon said that an old pub came into view:

> … but there was fast traffic behind me, so it was unsafe to turn. When I eventually went back to the spot, there was no such pub. A little further on, I visited a shop and described the building of natural stone, a large central door, ivy bound, and how I'd glanced a welcoming hearth fire glowing through the windows. The car park was empty of vehicles, and pebbled. I drove up and down this road for miles, because I couldn't believe it could literally vanish into thin air.

The elderly lady behind the counter confirmed that such a pub had existed 'back along some many years now,' she replied.

The Bottomless Pit

In the 1800s, John Knight of Worcester acquired the Royal Forest of Exmoor for £50,000. He decided to cultivate the waterish, boggy wasteland above Chain Barrow. Searchers of the supernatural have described the Chains as a place of great foreboding, just as scary in the day as after nightfall.

John Knight also established what today is called Pinkery Pond, sometimes known as Pinkworthy, an area of 7 acres with a pond 30-ft deep. No one knows why he created the pond, but embedded in the isolation of Exmoor rumours began to circulate of weird occurrences; ghostly riders on horseback, 'things' that murmur or stir at Flaxbarrow mound, flickering blue lights over the Whea Eliza mineshaft. Firm local advice warns never to visit this desolate place alone. Among its troubled spirits, the story of an ill-wishing wraith is still recalled. In 1906, whilst returning from the Chains to a farm where he was holidaying, a Mr Grey became confused as to which path to take. Much to his relief, a figure appeared. Grey called out for directions. In an instant, the figure faded. Guessing the safest route back, Grey struggled on only to fall into deep mud. He eventually arrived at the farm but soon caught a chill, which within hours turned into pneumonia. Luckily for him, he was nursed back to life by the farmer's mother. Grey told her about the strange figure, and her only comment was, 'Now 'ee do know who 'ee zeed up Pinkworthy'.

Pinkery Pond.

Taunton Tales

The famous 'hairy hands' said to clutch at travellers on the road to Princetown in Devon have a similar and to all accounts a very frightening rival on a stretch of moorland near Taunton. Nicknamed 'The One with the White Hand', the spirit has been variously described as a female, wearing white clothing that 'rustled like dead leaves', from which emerged a long thin hand to point a bony finger at whoever encountered her. Bodiless footsteps along cobbled lanes and strange whispers carried by the wind are some of the many Taunton tales to detonate the proverbial shivers.

The enchanting spires of Taunton are among the many welcome lights as the London to Penzance Express sighs into Somerset's charismatic county capital. Taunton is the integral hub and heart of Somerset's commercial world, whose encircling valleys are cider fruitful; along with leather, woollens, cattle and other agriculture, a feast of artistic activities in tandem with ghosts and ghouls who don't always hide their credentials. Although many of them are largely unrecorded, they frequently occur in the midst of coffee, club, pub or other social chat.

It is worth recapturing the town's potted but important history, much of which may be gleaned from Taunton's fine museum, which exhibits the relics of prehistoric activity, early British and Roman fragments, bullets and other weapons of Sedgemoor's great battle, and even a spy glass used from Chedzoy's Parish church tower to monitor the advancing Royalist army.

Caffe Nero at Taunton where Judge Jeffreys is supposed to wander.

The 'hanging judge', Judge Jeffreys, lists among Taunton's most infamous ghosts, and a host of Somerset pens have sought to describe his sentencing severities. The town centre's Caffe Nero, formerly the Tudor Restaurant, is included in his haunting habits, but it is at Taunton Castle where his bloodied decisions were given full vent. The Duke of Monmouth conquered Taunton Castle, and what became known as The Bloody Assizes opened in 1685, where, in the castle's Great Hall, hundreds of rebel soldiers were hauled before the merciless judge, and sentenced to death.

Considerable and controversial criticism has been played against the eye-witnessed recorded sadism of certain Army officers. Savage's *History of Taunton* pulls no punches in his vilification of Col. Percy Kirke, who hanged many prisoners without trial on their immediate arrival at Taunton:

> While the executioner was performing the mournful duties of his office, Kirke, with his customary barbarity, commanded the fifes to play, the trumpets to sound and the drums to beat, that the music might drown the cries of the dying victims and the lamentation of their relatives and the populace. The mangled bodies of these unfortunate men were, by his orders, immediately stripped, their breasts cleft asunder, and their hearts, while warm, separately thrown into a large fire: and as each was cast in, a great shout was raised, the executioner saying: 'there goes the heart of a traitor'. When they were burnt, their quarters were boiled in pitch and hung up at all crossways and public parts of the town and neighbourhood.

Taunton Castle archway – the sound of marching soldiers has been heard at this entranceway.

St Mary Magdelene, Taunton.

St Mary Magdalene's haunted churchyard.

These are appallingly evil atrocities by any standards, and it is unsurprising that, for whatever reasons, we hear of many restless spirits throughout the town, particularly at the castle.

Predictably, there has to be numerous occurrences of 'rebel soldiers'. It is claimed that at least a dozen victims were hung on the sign of the White Hart Inn, and their muffled cries have been heard ever since. On a stairway in the castle, a threatening, vapourish cavalier swiftly casts a threatening glance as he holds a sword in one hand and a pistol in the other. Close to High Street, the Crescent is inhabited by the alleged morganatic wife of George IV, who 'drifts' through walls or along the street, dressed in fabulous black silks. The hollow clatter of Monmouth's soldiers, tramping up the castle gate are another part of that terrible haunted page of history.

There is also an uneasy twist to St Mary Magdalene's old churchyard. The vicinity is acclaimed for ghostly faces, figures and presences. In 1883 Edward Goldsworthy in *Recollections of Old Taunton* wrote:

> A ghost story may not be inappropriate … The ghost was a very harmless one, but it scared the women and children terribly. A tall headstone had been placed in the churchyard, lancet-shaped on the top, with elevated corners looking not unlike arms partially raised. It was painted white, and varnished. Nothing was thought of or said about it until a gas-lamp was placed at the Post Office at the corner of Magdalene lane, the light from which was thrown over Church Square and some way up the churchyard. The effect of this light was to make the headstone appear at a distance like a human being with a sheet thrown over its head and shoulders. It did look ghastly at a distance, but not so when seen close.

Within a stone's throw from Taunton Gaol are Hammets Walk and the Wilton stream. Talking with long-rooted inhabitants produced vague recollections of the aura of a child hovering over the water and believed to have been murdered there.

AFTERWORD

I hope that every reader will become aware, though not too uncomfortably so, that personal beliefs in ghost lore, and its many unproven and psychological aspects, are never driven by blind faith. So, here we are again. We have returned full circle; sought and found places and situations occupied with ghosties and other characters filled with humour, mystery and suspense. The goal has been to present a glimpse into that irresistible thing called 'superstition.' Ghost hunters, sceptics, the curious and paranormal investigators will doubtless continue to come across other time-told tales and new sightings. Frequently, the will to believe in ghosts is compelling, and it is the wish of this author that enlightenment in this field will continue to grow and spur lucid discussion about a subject which is abstruse and too frequently misunderstood. In the belief of an elderly villager, 'Look for 'em? Look? Why look … they're all about you!'

Supernatural Somerset is an absorbing study and nowadays is developing into another frontier of tourism, with ghost hunts, clubs and explorer groups. It is tempting and easy to become mesmerised by the unknown; steeped as it is in the poetic beauty of Somerset's rapturous landscapes and the simple sweetness of thatch, green lanes, castle turrets and spectacular coast. To set foot in Somerset's haunting legends is inevitably to become truly immersed in the unique mystique of its ghostly heritage. Ghosts symbolise the past within the present; photo memories that serve to remind us of time's illusory realities, and in a sense can give reason to our transitory sojourn on planet ego.

BIBLIOGRAPHY

Author, collected anecdotes, interviews and private collection

Burrow, Edward J., *Ancient Earth Works and Camps of Somerset*, J. Burrow & Co. Ltd, London, (ed.) 1924

Burton, S.H., *A West Country Anthology*, Robert Hale, London, 1975

Dathen, Jon, *Somerset Cider Folklore and Customs*, Capall Bann Publishing, Somerset, 2006

Davies, Owen, *Witchcraft, Magic and Culture 1736–1951*, Manchester University Press, Manchester & New York, 1999

Delderfield, Eric R., *Exmoor Wanderings*, E.R.D. Publications, Exmouth, 1956

Garton, J.A., *Glowing Embers from a Somerset Hearth*, Clare, Son & Co. Ltd, Somerset, 1936

Gibbs, Ray, *Somerset Places and Legends*, Wales, 1991

Hann, A.C. Osborn, *Somerset*, A.&C. Black Co., London, 1927

Holt, Alan, *Folklore of Somerset*, Alan Sutton, Stroud, 1992

Hurley, Jack, *Legends of Exmoor*, The Exmoor Press, Dulverton, 1973

James, Tony, *Yankee Jack Sails Again*, Seafarer Books, Suffolk, 2006

Joyce, Walter W., *Moorside Tales and Talk*, George Allen & Unwin Ltd, London, 1935

Lawrence, Berta, *A Somerset Journal*, Westaway Books, London, 1951

Lawrence, Berta, *Quantock Country*, Westaway Books, London, 1952

Leete-Hodge, Lornie, *Curiosities of Somerset*, Bossiney Books, Cornwall, 1985

Pevsner, Nikolaus, *The Buildings of England South and West Somerset*, Penguin Books, Middlesex, 1958

Somerset & Dorset, Notes & Queries, Vols. 1–5, XVIII, 1912–13, 1930–32, Sherborne

Somerset Reviewer, various volumes, Somerset

Somerset Yearbook, The, Folk Press Limited, London, 1923–36

Tongue, Ruth, *Somerset Folklore*, The Folklore Society, London, 1965

Underwood, Peter, *Ghosts of Somerset*, Bossiney Books, Cornwall, 1965

Wade, G.W. & J.H., *Rambles in Somerset*, Methuen, London, 1912

Waite, Vincent, *Portrait of the Quantocks*, Robert Hale Ltd, London, 1964

West Country Magazine, various

Whynne-Hammon, Charles, *Ten Somerset Mysteries*, Countryside Books, Berkshire, 1995

Other local titles published by The History Press

Haunted Bristol
SUE LE' QUEUX

This enthralling selection of newspaper reports and first-hand accounts recalls strange and spooky happenings in the city's ancient streets, churches, theatres and public houses, including the Rummer pub and the White Hart, which has seen plenty of poltergeist activity! It is a unique glimpse into the ghostly legacy of Bristol's past that is sure to appeal to anyone interested in a spot of ghost-hunting.

978 0 7524 3300 4

Haunted Devon
IAN ADDICOAT

From the ghost of Isabella, the illegitimate child of Baron de Pomeroy murdered when she was but nine, to séances at the Smuggler's Haunt, personal messages from Peggy Penny and a ghost tour around Boringdon Hall, this phenomenal gathering of ghostly goings-on is bound to captivate anyone interested in the supernatural history of the area.

978 0 7524 3977 8

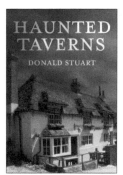

Haunted Taverns
DONALD STUART

From hair-raising tales about a fourteenth-century pub with its own ghost duck, the phantom who leaves a strong smell of rum and tobacco throughout an ancient inn, the beer jug that fills itself up in the middle of the night to a Devil's dog the size of a calf that disappears into the walls of the old inn it haunts, this book will bring goose-bumps to those who dare to open its cover.

978 0 7524 4347 8

Somerset Dragons
BRIAN WRIGHT

This fascinating exploration of dragon lore in Somerset is a useful guide to the many representations of dragons that can be seen in the county, from ancient carvings on church walls and pew ends to stained-glass windows and modern dragons on contemporary architecture.

978 0 7524 2606 8

If you are interested in purchasing other books published by The History Press, or in case you have difficulty finding any of our books in your local bookshop, you can also place orders directly through our website
www.thehistorypress.co.uk